A PATCH OF GREEN

A Patch of Green

CANADA'S OILPATCH MAKES PEACE WITH THE ENVIRONMENT

Sydney Sharpe

KEY PORTER BOOKS

National Library of Canada Cataloguing in Publication Data

Sharpe, Sydney
A patch of green : Canada's oilpatch makes peace with the environment / Sydney Sharpe.

Includes bibliographical references and index.
ISBN 1-55263-520-1

1. Petroleum industry and trade—Environmental aspects—Canada. 2. Gas industry—Environmental aspects—Canada. I. Title.

HD9574.C22S52 2002   333.8'23'0971   C2002-904255-0

THE CANADA COUNCIL | LE CONSEIL DES ARTS
FOR THE ARTS | DU CANADA
SINCE 1957 | DEPUIS 1957

ONTARIO ARTS COUNCIL
CONSEIL DES ARTS DE L'ONTARIO

The publisher gratefully acknowledges the support of the Canada Council for the Arts and the Ontario Arts Council for its publishing program.

We acknowledge the financial support of the Government of Canada through the Book Publishing Industry Development Program (BPIDP) for our publishing activities.

Key Porter Books Limited
70 The Esplanade
Toronto, Ontario
Canada M5E 1R2

www.keyporter.com

Cover design: Peter Maher
Electronic formatting: Heidi Palfrey

Printed and bound in Canada

02 03 04 05 06 07 6 5 4 3 2 1

This book is dedicated to the late Judy Wish-Hamilton,
whose courage, diplomacy, and tenacity
made her a model, mentor, and trailblazer
in the oilpatch and in politics.
Countless friends will always treasure her memory.

Contents

Acknowledgements

More than 100 people generously consented to be interviewed for this book. Workers within the oil and gas industry, from CEO to consultant, shared their time and knowledge so that I could fully understand the profound changes that have occurred. Environmentalists, from inside and outside the oilpatch, presented their critiques, concerns and kudos, while academics and commentators provided their insight. I am truly indebted to all of them, although any errors in appreciation and presentation are fully my responsibility.

My deepest thanks go first to my daughter Rielle Braid, my son Gabriel Cardenas-Sharpe, and my husband Don Braid for putting up with deadline demands and author angst.

My wonderful friend Norah Hutchinson gave up her computer at a crucial time, while also providing her perspective. Dr. Richard Heyman and Ms. Phoebe Heyman generated passionate debate over dinner on Kyoto and climate change.

My understanding of the regulatory network was greatly enhanced by journalist and communications consultant Lisa Monforton, who pored through acres of government documents and offered her knowledge and ideas.

Martha Kostuch brought her enthusiasm, experience, and dedication as an environmentalist to our discussions and helped me fully appreciate her impact and goals.

Beth Diamond urged me on with her insights into the industry, and I thank her enormously. David Carson gave me his thoughts as one who has toiled both within and outside the oilpatch. Barbara Camponi brought her adventurous life to bear on appreciating the frontier nature of exploration and development.

I am indebted to veteran journalist Patrick Nagel for his wisdom and knowledge, as I am also to consultants Jock Osler and Jim Stanton.

Thanks to Louise O'Hora, who helped me juggle what seemed like an insurmountable task into a manageable process. Michel-André Roy and Jean Williams transformed administrative tangles into reasonable targets. Arthur Darby offered his skill as an editor, which I commandeered with gratitude for the bibliography.

Special thanks goes to Anna Porter, Clare McKeon, Sue Sumeraj, and Janie Yoon of Key Porter Books, who helped my idea become "A Patch of Green."

Introduction

As the national quarrel over the Kyoto Protocol escalates, no industry is under more critical scrutiny than oil and gas. The petroleum business is blamed for exploiting fossil fuels, polluting the land and air where it operates, causing the greenhouse gas problem, and generally contributing to global warming. Many Canadians seem to believe that if oil and gas companies are forced to curb their excesses, the climate itself will be cured.

Most of the criticism is false, or at least wildly exaggerated, but there's nothing new about it. In 1994, when I started writing about oil and gas as Calgary bureau chief of the *Financial Post*, I realized almost immediately that the industry was a handy punching bag for a whole bundle of hostile interests.

Yet the reality of the business failed miserably to fit its stereotype. The "oilpatch," as it's commonly called, was full of rambunctious characters who were frankly out to get rich, but who knew that a new set of rules had emerged. No longer could the environment be casually pillaged as it had been in the days when oil companies (and most other industrial businesses) didn't worry about the mess they left behind. Modern oil companies are much more careful with their neighbours, with Aboriginals, and with the air and water around their operations. Some companies and employees enthusiastically embrace the new ethic. Others follow along because they know the risks of flouting laws and public opinion, but follow they do.

After Kyoto was endorsed by the Canadian government in 1997, and the slow march to ratification began, the industry launched another wave of environmental action and rapid improvement. With surprising speed, a creaky old industry had modernized both its mind and its machinery, and roared past many others toward the millennium. Today the Canadian oilpatch can boast of remarkable advances in environmental technology and practice, and in its dealings with many interest groups. Critical but knowledgeable environmentalists admit they're impressed, almost in spite of themselves.

Yet the public's awareness of these changes lagged far behind the reality all through the 1990s. It still does today. The oil and gas business is portrayed in many media as an uncaring polluter with no regard for the environment. Part of this attitude stems from ignorance about what the companies and regulators are actually doing. More of it grows from the ideological conviction that no matter how clean the industry becomes, it still has no right to exist because it uses fossil fuels. For these opponents, it is legitimate to try to discredit the industry on the slimmest pretext. What's more, blunders and arrogance on the part of some international oil companies, such as Exxon in Alaska and Royal Dutch/Shell in Nigeria, have done the rest of the industry no good. Yet these companies have also shown that they can change for the better.

In Canada, the Wiebo Ludwig affair became the focus of vitriolic anti-industry sentiment in the late 1990s. Even though Ludwig's charges of environmental and health damage were contradictory and unsupported by evidence, his story was swallowed whole by many Canadians. His criminal convictions related to bombings seemed to make little difference to this perception. The targets of bombings—the companies and people who worked for them—somehow became the villains.

The obvious unfairness of this situation nudged me toward writing this book. Later, the promise of cooperation from environmentalists, Aboriginals, academics, regulators, and key industry leaders made me determined to do it. My brief time working in a senior position at an integrated oil company gave me valuable insight into the seriousness with which concerned companies tackle environmental challenges.

I've tried to set out a clear picture of how the industry handles emissions, pollution and social concerns, both in Canada and abroad. The inescapable conclusion is that, while problems remain, the successes are remarkable.

Environmental scientists are convincing the companies that employ them to make projects green and clean, or to abandon them entirely. Executives who were once casual polluters have become avid environmentalists. Native leaders explain how an industry that once ignored or exploited them now takes their concerns seriously, bringing benefits to their people and communities. Industry leaders show how their opposition to the Kyoto Accord is consistent with both environmentalism and sound economics. And the people who live near Wiebo Ludwig finally get to tell their side of the story, which directly contradicts his.

Radical critics of the industry may find that this book challenges their beliefs. As always, facts can be inconvenient to dogma. That dilemma is theirs to ponder; my role is simply to set out the evidence.

The Patch

C hief Jim Boucher's Fort MacKay Native band lives near one of the biggest oil projects in the world, the surface mining of the vast oilsands at Fort McMurray, Alberta. His band has seen its way of life changed radically over past decades by the birth and rapid growth of these mammoth industrial operations. The sense of loss is palpable among people whose cultural memory runs lightly along the paths of many centuries.

But Boucher, like other Native leaders today, has made his wary peace with the oil and gas business. Many members of his band now feel that the mining companies, often reviled as the most intrusive environmental offenders in the oil business, are in fact more sensitive to both culture and environment than other industries in Canada. The conclusion is not unique to Boucher's band. Indeed, it reflects the industry's quiet growth from casual polluter in its early days to its new role as a vigilant, and occasionally militant, steward of the environment.

"When the first oilsands plant was constructed on our territory in the 1960s, the effects were immediate," Boucher says. "People lost hunting grounds, berry-picking areas, and waterfowl. Some families were displaced. There were concerns over water quality, air quality, and health and safety of animals. The development brought an influx of people into the area and we had to compete for natural resources. There were intrusions by government, in the form of regulations and laws which circumvented our ways to make a living."[1]

In the 1980s, environmentalists themselves dealt a blow to the old way of life by attacking Native hunting and fishing rights.

"This most important cornerstone of our lifestyle was taken from the people," Boucher recalls sadly. "The motivation was no longer there. That's why our people were thrown into social chaos. All of a sudden we had nothing to do."

With the band's very survival at stake, leaders like Boucher, who has been chief since 1986, decided to try something new and radical—cooperation with the industry. And the oil executives, sick of costly hearings, conflict, personal unpopularity, and streams of bad publicity, were quick to respond.

Boucher says: "Since that decision was made to cooperate with industry, we've begun to address many environmental issues. Emission levels, specifically of sulphur, were reduced by Suncor and Syncrude, and they've installed naphtha recovery technology and capped their tanks." Huge stretches of mined land are also being reclaimed and restored.

Once an adversary, Boucher now sounds like a champion of the industry. "There has been a positive engagement in terms of specific environmental concerns," he says. "The industry's leadership is exemplary in comparison with what goes on across the country. This industry leads in environmental issues. It has developed new technologies to ensure environmental concerns are being met."

Boucher is also convinced that the oil business is far more generous than other Canadian industries in providing jobs, programs, and economic benefits to Natives affected by their operations. This is true not just in Canada, but in many places where Canadian firms operate abroad. One example is EnCana Corp.'s stake in Ecuador, where the giant company invests heavily in education, training, and social programs for local people.

Joyce Metchewais, Chief of Alberta's Cold Lake First Nation, was impressed when she visited EnCana's Ecuadorean operations in 2000 (the firm was then known as Alberta Energy Company). Her own band had just signed a $10-million joint venture deal with Alberta Energy and Precision Drilling Corporation, under which the band, with others, bought and operated its own drilling rig. "We're tired of sitting on the sidelines watching the world go past us," Metchewais said then. "It's good that industry is recognizing we're capable of this kind of venture." To the Natives in Ecuador she said, "Don't let anyone tell you what's good for you. We can't sit back and let others make our own decisions for us."[2]

To an unprecedented extent, companies are inviting Natives to join them as partners both in oil and gas operations and in environmental protection. Bands everywhere give them credit for changes that are rarely publicized.

"The companies have gone far beyond what was done in the 1960s, '70s, and '80s," says Boucher. "Back then they would decide what they were going to do and then defend their project. Now they work with communities in a positive way. This is a major shift."

These views run counter to the image of the oil industry as insensitive in the places where it drills, pumps, and mines, and uncaring about pollution wherever its products are sold and used. Many stereotypes are at least 20 years out of date, but in Canada they are perpetuated by radical environmentalists who have an outmoded notion of Big Oil, and by a national media system based outside the producing areas of Alberta, British Columbia, Saskatchewan, Newfoundland, and Nova Scotia.

Jim Boucher and many others who live alongside the oil companies are quick to add that their neighbours are far from perfect. Some operators, especially smaller ones, would simply walk away from their used-up wells if they could get away with it (and a few manage to). Needless flares of natural gas still dot the night landscapes in Alberta, although far fewer than there were in the 1980s, when, seen from the air, the flares looked like torches carried by the soldiers of vast advancing armies.

When the oil companies began to change in the 1980s, many didn't do so willingly. They were forced out of their old habits by protests, legal rulings, and regulatory scoldings. They had been casual about land and water pollution; the air, according to Edmonton lawyer Jerome Slavik, was treated as "a common dumping ground."

Slavik, who has represented Aboriginals in their conflicts with the oil industry for many years, is scathing about the companies' earlier practices, both environmental and cultural.

"In the 1960s, '70s, and early '80s in the oilsands, industry ignored the presence, interests, and concerns of Aboriginals whether they were social, economic, or environmental.

"Natives just weren't on the radar screen. Initially, they were ignored because they weren't thought to be an issue; then they were ignored because the industry didn't know how to deal with them; then the industry tried to avoid them.

"Only when the conflicts were clear, and in the face of direct legal and political impediments, did the companies get serious and address the issues in creative and inclusive ways."[3]

The same dynamic applied not just to Natives, but to the industry's dealings with non-Native communities and the environment. Companies were casual at best in relations with farmers and ranchers who owned the land where they exploited their mineral leases. They downplayed and at times ignored complaints about the flaring of natural gas, even of dangerous sour gas, rich in poisonous hydrogen sulphide.

But once the oil and gas industry began to change, and the companies realized that money could still be made—indeed, that environmental improvements could eventually save money—the best companies became advocates for still more change. The green movement within the industry snowballed through the 1990s as companies hired environmental scientists who developed stringent environmental rules.

Today, some of Canada's keenest environmentalists work inside the oil companies, where they have new status and influence. Company executives know that if they ignore environmental advice, they face a sharp backlash from regulators, shareholders, and the public. The best corporate environmentalists clean up and prevent more damage in a month than the protestors may ever achieve. Yet they are routinely castigated as sellouts by people whose basic values they share.

Skeptical observers like Jerome Slavik recognize the changes and give the industry full credit. "The image is still of a rapacious, insensitive industry, but today's reality is quite different," Slavik says. "There have been huge improvements."

"Environment is much more central to business decision-making and corporate strategy than it used to be," says Gordon Lambert, vice-president of sustainable development at Suncor. "In the past it was a peripheral element of the business, but that has changed."[4] Adds Rick George, Suncor's chief executive officer: "Most leaders in the oilpatch are family men; they've got children, and they worry about the future as much as anyone else does."[5]

Yet the perception of industry wrongdoing is deeply rooted outside the West and other producing regions. Everyone recognizes that Ontario's auto industry is central to the national economy, but the petroleum business gets scarce credit for being crucial, not just to the auto and manufacturing industries, but to Canadian prosperity. There is little understanding of petroleum's social and economic contribution to the country (500,000 people employed and $25 billion in investment in 2001, when the oil and gas trade surplus accounted for nearly 50 per cent of Canada's trade balance).[6] The economic benefits spread far beyond the producing regions. Anticipating the development of Mackenzie delta natural gas, Northwest Territories premier Stephen Kakfwi says that for every dollar of economic output in the NWT, 19 cents will be generated in Ontario.[7]

To some critics, the fossil-fuel industry itself is untenable and should simply fade into history at the earliest possible moment. Even moderate environmentalists like Alberta's Martha Kostuch, who often opposes the industry but also works with it, says: "In 50 years there should be no consumption of fossil fuels for energy in the world."[8] It's an increasingly common view that the industry will have to deal with.

"There is a faction in the environmental community that believes oil and gas is inherently bad, that it's not sustainable and only creates pollution," says Greta Raymond, Petro-Canada's vice-president of human resources, environment, health, and safety. "I think it's obvious that we provide more positive benefits, but it's hard to get away from that image."[9]

This is especially difficult as national debate focuses on the Kyoto Accord, which commits signatories to reducing carbon dioxide emissions. Many proposals would thrust the main burden—or penalty—on oil-and-gas–producing regions, an approach that perversely ignores both environmental and economic realities.

The production of oil and gas releases only a relatively small portion of the carbon dioxide—less than 20 per cent—produced in Canada by the use of hydrocarbons. The consumption of those petroleum products creates fully 80 per cent, and most of that is released in populous places like Toronto, Montreal, and Vancouver, far from the oil and gas wells.

A federal government report released in August 2002 stated, "It will be difficult to find a way to meet Canada's Kyoto target without significant action to reduce emissions from the transportation sector. This sector, counting both passenger and freight, is now the largest source [of greenhouse gas] emissions and is growing more rapidly than any other."[10]

Charlie Fischer, the CEO of senior producer Nexen Inc., is blunt about the apparent hypocrisy of attacks on producing regions of the country. "People like to hurl insults at the industry about this stuff, but the consumer vehicle of choice is the sport utility vehicle. Over a 10-year period, the sale of cars went up marginally, while truck sales went up dramatically, due to SUVs."[11]

Greta Raymond of Petro-Canada says, "It really is a consumption issue, but the rhetoric in the system leads people to believe there's a solution where they as consumers don't have to participate. Because we produce the oil and gas, we're somehow expected to produce the solution too."

Environment Canada, not always a friend to the industry, notes the real source of the CO_2 problem in its own reports. Cars are responsible for 60 per cent of national emissions of carbon dioxide, carbon monoxide, and other compounds, the agency says. And the shift from cars to larger vehicles, mainly SUVs, is responsible for 45 per cent of the increase in emissions since 1990.

Commenting on these findings, the federal U.S. Energy Information Administration said in April 2002: "Although Canada has benefited from fuel efficiency technologies over the same time period [since 1990], improvements have not been great enough to compensate for the increasing popularity of SUVs." The American report notes that "SUVs also produce, on average, one-third more carbon dioxide per mile than the average passenger car."[12]

Hypocrisy on the subject extends well beyond our borders to the heart of Europe. On April 14, 2002, when G-8 environment ministers were meeting in Banff, the German minister, Jurgen Trittin, saw too many SUVs for his taste.[13] They are indeed popular in the mountain town, where snow can hit even in summer—but many of the four-wheel-drive vehicles Trittin saw were certainly produced by German companies like BMW and Mercedes. Porsche, an even more exclusive German brand, is also coming out with an SUV.

On the international stage, Canada is subject to a rampant double standard that ignores our vast northern geography. Even the Americans scold us for producing more carbon per dollar of GDP than they do (although less than Mexico). Canada is scorned for consuming more energy per capita than Europe, but hardly anybody notes that our carbon rating is better than that of many OECD countries. The reason for this, as the American report is forced to note, is "the country's relatively low reliance on carbon-intensive coal and greater dependence on hydroelectricity and nuclear power (which do not emit carbon) and natural gas (which emits relatively little carbon)." We consume a great deal of energy in Canada but produce less greenhouse gas than we might—and the petroleum industry actually helps us accomplish this. Our exports of clean natural gas also help the Americans, but the Chrétien government failed to negotiate any credit for this in the original Kyoto Protocol, and now the Europeans adamantly resist it.

Canadians are but dimly aware that if any Kyoto-like agreement imposes serious economic disadvantages on our oil and gas industry, many companies could quickly slip into the hands of U.S. investors. Kyoto would drive down the value of Canadian firms, thus making them more tempting targets for American companies that would be under no such handicaps. Americans already enjoy an investment advantage because of their strong dollar. By giving them yet another economic edge, Kyoto would rapidly escalate a recent takeover trend that has seen major producers like Anderson Exploration and Canadian Hunter fall into the hands of big American firms.

"Canadian companies would be hit very hard by any disadvantage," says Murray Edwards, a Calgary oil investor, financier, and industrialist who's also an ardent federal Liberal and strong Canadian nationalist. "We could end up with U.S. domination of the Canadian oil and gas industry—that's very possible. Kyoto would definitely make the Canadian oil and gas industry vulnerable to U.S. companies."[14]

Another possibility is that investment, both Canadian and American, would flee Canada at a time when huge injections of capital are needed to develop projects in Canada's north, the oilsands, and the east coast. The irony is that at a time when the United States is focusing on energy sufficiency, Canada may drive investment dollars away.

Such points are obviously of vital importance to Canada. Far more beguiling to the mainstream media, however, are sensational stories like the bombings and sabotage of wells and other company installations in northern Alberta in the 1990s. Wiebo Ludwig, who claimed that oilpatch pollution was poisoning his family and caused a stillbirth, was sentenced on April 26, 2000, to 28 months in prison for five counts of possessing explosives, counselling possession, and destroying property. An innocent girl, 16-year-old Karman Willis, was shot to death on Ludwig's land during the conflict. Nobody has ever been charged with the killing.

In another high-profile case, tried several months after Ludwig was convicted, central Alberta rancher Wayne Roberts was convicted of shooting oilman Patrick Kent to death on his property and was sentenced to 15 years in penitentiary. The two men had a five-year history of escalating conflict over a contaminated well on Roberts's land.

Ludwig got wide attention for his claims of industry poisoning, yet the convincing evidence against his charges was rarely mentioned. Somehow, it was considered justifiable that people who professed to campaign against pollution could condone explosions that released deadly hydrogen sulphide gas into the atmosphere, forcing road closures and evacuations. The sheer terror unleashed among residents of Alberta's Peace River country was incidental to a holy crusade against the industry.

Like every resource industry in Canada, from mining to forestry, fishing, and even farming, the oil and gas business has much to answer for. In its early days it was a rampant polluter and later it resisted reform. Today, however, the industry is arguably cleaner than any of the others and improving. That story surely deserves attention as the industry comes under still more uninformed pressure that could severely damage Canada's economy.

CHAPTER TWO

The Shift

W hen Gwyn Morgan was a kid back on his family's central Alberta farm in the 1960s, he didn't think about the environment very much. In fact, the boy who grew up to be one of Canada's most dedicated corporate environmentalists now realizes that he was a casual polluter, just like nearly everyone else in Canada.

"On the farm we didn't think of ourselves as polluters, but we were," says Morgan, now the CEO of EnCana Corp., the largest Canadian-owned oil and gas company and the country's biggest industrial concern.

"In fact, we were terrible polluters. . . . It was just one of those things that everybody did. I often thought I did more damage as a farm kid than I ever could have done in the oil industry."[1]

Farmers in Alberta, and all over Canada, casually dumped manure near groundwater, seldom thought about how they disposed of chemicals, and didn't worry much about the dangers of pollutants to animals or humans. They were typical of the whole population. Those were the days when environmentalism wasn't even a word and consumers echoed the bad habits of corporations. Recycling of household waste was unknown. Suburbanites burned leaves on their front lawns, flushed soap into sewers as they washed their cars, and even sluiced oil down drains when they gave the family car an oil and filter change in the driveway.

The industrial companies, meanwhile, were blithely poisoning the Love Canal, killing fish in Hamilton Bay, spreading acid rain across Ontario, ripping out magnificent B.C. forests with no thought of replanting, and scarring prairie landscapes in search of oil. In the petroleum business, workers often sprayed waste oil to kill weeds at tank batteries and other installations. As the industry grew, huge volumes of natural gas were flared off, and seismic crews cut swaths of forest without thought to the impact on wildlife or neighbours.

Gwyn Morgan saw the pollution from many angles, because his family's farm was right next to a dirty petroleum installation. "My first exposure to the oil industry was on our farm, about half a mile downwind from one of Alberta's first really significant sour gas plants, west of Carstairs. . . . In those days the technology of sulphur dioxide recovery wasn't so advanced. Ninety per cent was considered good. Now it's more than 99 per cent. . . . I mean, there must have been a pretty high concentration coming off that plant. Compared to today, it was probably a hundred times more on a concentration basis. And we were downwind of this thing."

Nobody thought much about the health risks, although they hated the rotten-egg smell from the dangerous hydrogen sulphide in the gas—anybody would. This is one of the most offensive odours released by any industrial process on the planet. But, like everyone else in the community, Morgan tried to ignore it because of the economic benefits. "A lot of local kids were being employed there, so we thought it was a good thing," he recalls.

Morgan also saw the lack of respect petroleum companies often demonstrated toward landowners: "We were in one of these areas where companies wanted to drill, so we'd have seismic crews leaving gates open and cutting fences. I'd have to round up the cattle. That was my exposure to the oil industry in the early days.

"I think the oil industry certainly was no worse than any business sector or the farming sector or anything else in terms of its environmental impact. But we have learned a whole bunch, and there's no doubt about that."

In his youth, Morgan probably put up with far more pollution and annoyance than energy companies ever caused for Wiebo Ludwig's clan in the Peace River area. People like Morgan, and the environmental staff they employ, do as much good for the environment as the radicals, although the best of them acknowledge that constant pressure forces energy companies to set ever higher goals.

Today, the industry is in the latter stages of a massive paradigm shift. Every reputable company strives to operate with the least possible damage to the environment, and the ones that still slide around the rules come in for corporate shunning and regulatory scolding. The rigid old notion of the bottom line—profit above everything—has been replaced by the more complex concept of the "triple bottom line." In this model, companies are judged not just on profit, but also on their environmental and social performance.

Most do it not because they're pure and noble. The petroleum business, like any other, exists to sell a product and make money for owners and shareholders, but they now realize that environmental responsibility is an integral part of economic success. "Most companies are recognizing that if they are going to be profitable in the long run, they have to attend to environmental and public issues—I don't see it as pure altruism," says pioneer Alberta regulator George Govier.[2]

Neither does veteran oilpatch observer Jeff Jones, Calgary bureau chief for Reuters, the international news agency. "This is an industry that has been pulled kicking and screaming into having to count environmental issues as part of their day-to-day operations," he says. "They continue to kick and scream, but they're doing it." Like Govier, Jones doesn't see altruism as much of a motivator.[3]

Govier recalls that there was always some budding environmental concern, even back in the 1950s and 1960s. "That was one of the things being considered back then; the emphasis had gradually changed already." But in those days, immense profits could still be made by companies that ignored or casually damaged the environment. Today that's impossible, because "environmental liability" will almost always catch up with a careless or cynical company.

Wilf Gobert, a top analyst with oilpatch investment banker Peters & Co., recalls a case where flouting environmental laws literally destroyed the value of an oil company.

"Bids for properties are subject to environmental assessment," Gobert says. "One buyer ended up concluding that the cost of an environmental cleanup if his company bought the land of another was too high, so he dumped the deal."[4]

The company trying to sell had failed to build a berm, or low wall, around a battery of oil storage tanks. Such berms are required by regulation to contain any oil spills. The small company virtually destroyed itself by failing to do the work. Gobert says, "The deal fell apart because the environmental liability made the assets almost worthless. . . . Today, the poor environmental reputation of a company can dramatically affect the value because the marketplace won't own its stock."

The new ethic has percolated from head offices down to the field, where the consequences of polluting can bring instant firing.

"One summer I worked for an oil pipeline company in the States, and we would run pigs," recalls Rick George, now the CEO of integrated oil company Suncor. (Pigs are devices used to test the integrity of pipelines, so called because they emit an electronic squeal.) "You would always end up with a couple of buckets of oil when you took the pig out, and we'd bleed that off and kill the weeds in the area around. Today you would get fired for that—and it was a kind of standard operating procedure. The attitudes and approaches have just moved miles."[5]

George has three goals for his Suncor employees and himself: to improve efficiency, reduce the costs of producing oil, and eliminate environmental damage. "You try to do all three things in the safest manner possible, and if every employee does that, then you're going to have a very successful company." As a hard-headed businessman, George knows that taking on projects that don't pay is "a good way to be a CEO for about six months." But the best environmental practices do pay in the short term, and they can also avert major costs later on.

"Taking [environmental] shortcuts never helps you. When you're trying to develop a gas plant or a plant up north in the oilsands or a pipeline, you know it's better to do it with the best technology and the best means you can, when you first put those things in. Because if you have to go back and retrofit it five years later, that is so much more costly. So there are no shortcuts. You use the best technology in the best way possible because reworking and retrofitting is so difficult."

Gwyn Morgan now considers himself an ardent environmentalist who runs a company full of like-minded people. A fitness buff who exercises daily, Morgan says, "I bet I do a lot more activities, hike more miles in the mountains, and spend more time in the outdoors than 99 per cent of these people who think they're environmentalists." He resents any implication that people are uncaring about the environment just because they work for an oil company. "Our people live in every community where we have operations, and they want a clean environment too. The people of EnCana are every bit as concerned about the environment as our neighbours are." For Morgan the mission is both practical and ideological. "I've got this perspective that the success of the free enterprise system is based on demonstrating it is better than any other one. I look at the socialist countries and former communist countries where the government did everything, and in every single case, the environment is a disaster.

"In Ecuador, where the biggest operator is still the government, for years we have been cleaning up the rainforest from stuff they left behind. Today, our environmental practices in that country are on a whole different tier than their national oil company. In fact, their environment minister told me that."

Alejandro Suarez, Ecuador's ambassador to Canada, told me that EnCana's commitment to the Ecuadorian people and the environment was exemplary, and he commended EnCana and its employees for their performance.[6]

Despite this, radical environmental organizations have been conducting a campaign to discredit EnCana's operation in Ecuador. Morgan finds this annoying and unfair. He says his company uses the same environmental standards abroad as at home, and "there's no doubt that the upstream oil and gas industry in Alberta is one of the cleanest of any kind in the world."

Nexen Inc. CEO Charlie Fischer also insists that his company has no double standard when it operates abroad. "We don't differentiate between one part of the world and another. We apply the same standards everywhere we work, whether countries themselves have standards or not. We do it because the capability is there.

"The industry has always been conscious of the environment, but today the science around environment has developed significantly and regulations have been adjusted dramatically.

"You don't see flare pits anymore. Cleanups on well sumps are dramatically different than before. Emissions standards are much stronger regarding hydrogen sulphide. In general, there's a lot more focus and understanding. When I started in the business, I don't recall companies even having environment departments. Today they are integrated with the operating groups."[7]

In the early days of dawning oil company awareness, those environmentalists were often hired for window dressing, and they knew it. That's uncommon today. Gordon Lambert, Suncor's vice-president of sustainable development, works at the company's highest level and has his CEO's enthusiastic confidence. Rick George says, "He has pushed this company, and me, further than what seemed possible. Gord has got job security. He's two doors away from my office."

For Lambert, sustainable development embraces the company's social, environmental, and economic performance—the triple bottom line. "I see that as a growing trend," he says. "There are really two drivers. The first is the example of firms that have done poorly at earning community trust or credibility and have paid the price for it, whether in project delays or adversarial licence processes or straight community outrage.

"On the flip side, where companies use their environmental and social performance strategically, there are positive examples of what that means for shareholder value."[8]

With tighter government regulations and citizens determined to see them enforced, companies have one goal when they want to build projects—to avoid costly and adversarial public hearings. This means much more consultation in advance of building anything. Companies like Suncor pride themselves on managing to stay out of the hearing room. "In our case," says Lambert, "we haven't had adversarial hearings on our growing projects, because we've been able to deal with stakeholder concerns outside hearings." The savings can be enormous. One law partnership promises to save firms millions of dollars, if not tens of millions, by helping companies avoid hearings.

One company executive after another describes huge changes over recent decades. "I have been working in this business for over 20 years, and when I reflect back, I think that changes in attitude and relationships have been significant," says Kathy Sendall, Petro-Canada's senior vice-president for Western Canada. "When I started out as an engineer designing and constructing projects, I think we rarely considered the environmental impact of our activities. The mantra tended to be 'get it done, fast and cheap.' Environmental assessments were not exactly the norm."[9]

Today, she says, "the industry is significantly more sensitive. . . . Environmental issues are clearly part of the business agenda, and are well integrated into the daily business management systems. Business leaders are now held as accountable for decisions and performance on environmental matters as for any other business decision." Like most major companies, Petro-Can has its own environmental management system, which conforms to the International Standard on environmental management.

Companies also talk about their "licence to operate"—and they don't mean technical approvals from government. They're referring to the goodwill generated by sound operations within a community. "You must safeguard the local environment in order to preserve your licence to operate with the community," says Sendall. "This licence means more than just regulatory approval; it means building positive, respectful relationships with the people and communities in the vicinity of your facilities."

Former Enbridge Inc. CEO Brian MacNeill says his company spent endless time talking to communities about pipeline safety. "We've got people every 40 miles from here to Montreal out there educating the communities. We do a lot of family safety nights. It's an ongoing education process, and at the end of the day there's a benefit to it for everyone. There's a cost to accidents and environmental breaches. To prevent them is just good business practice."[10] Behind much of this is the obvious reality that if the industry doesn't police itself, governments will. This became more obvious to the oil and gas business than to many others when the federal government gave preliminary approval to the Kyoto Protocol in 1997.

To industry leaders, it was immediately obvious that the burden of reducing carbon dioxide emissions could fall heavily on petroleum producers. They remember their history very well—especially the National Energy Program of 1980—and understand that the federal government is always more likely to penalize Western industries than Central Canadian ones. The industry set out to make this as difficult as possible for Ottawa by accelerating the pace of environmental improvement.

"Industry wants to be masters of their own change and there has been a growing awareness of what governments can do if they take over," says Irene Pfeiffer, president of PWR Search, which places many oil industry executives. "The general public is better educated and more concerned about their environment and is making its views known through the media, public meetings, and protests. The status quo is no longer acceptable."[11]

The Canadian Association of Petroleum Producers (CAPP), the companies' blanket organization, is an increasingly active player in the industry's sea change. A decade ago it worked with governmental, environmental, and other agencies to establish the Clean Air Strategic Alliance (CASA), which encourages the industry to attack pollution by reducing flaring and other practices. "It was regarded as a novel, somewhat scary vehicle, but everyone had a commitment to make it work," says CAPP vice-president David Pryce.[12] The initiative improved relations with landowners (although conflicts remain and probably always will).

In the late 1990s CAPP began the Environment Health and Safety Stewardship Program, a voluntary grouping of companies dedicated to following best practices. The impact on flaring has been remarkable—it's down 53 per cent, exceeding even the most optimistic targets. In 2002 CAPP made participation in the stewardship program mandatory for members, starting in January 2003. One of CAPP's goals, says Pryce, is to give a competitive advantage to companies that respect the environment. "We want the public and the regulator to recognize the value of the program and to challenge non-participating companies to commit to the program," he says.[13] CAPP has also been instrumental in creating and paying for the Orphan Well Fund, which cleans up wells left environmentally unsound by insolvent or disbanded companies.

CAPP president Pierre Alvarez, once a top aide to Senator Pat Carney when she was federal energy minister, says CAPP is dedicated to improving the industry's performance and image. He sees major changes everywhere. "Historically, the industry always fought the science," Alvarez says. "Now the industry is prepared to say there are some issues where science may be uncertain, but they recognize serious issues. Then there's the willingness to bring third-party stakeholders into the process. The days of 'I'm the expert' are over. Despite the fact that companies have an overriding legal licence to develop the mineral resources, they recognize the importance of the landowners' rights, and those of First Nations."[14]

Nowhere is the potential for conflict greater than around the oilsands projects of Fort McMurray. Mining oilsands uses more energy than any other type of oil production, and therefore produces more greenhouse gas. The oilsands process is more like heavy industrial production—making steel or smelting aluminum—than collecting oil and gas from drilled wells. But with conventional oil depleting, the sands, which contain more oil than Saudi Arabia's reserves, are vital to Canada's future supplies.

Eric Newell, CEO of Syncrude, the largest oilsands producer, gives an idea of the impact on the town and Native communities. "Never in the history of Canada," he says, "has a community the size of Fort McMurray had to bear the brunt of a $50-billion investment."[15]

Newell was an ardent environmentalist long before many of his colleagues in the industry began to see the green. As a young engineer in England, he worked with Sir Frederick Warner, who was knighted for his work in cleaning up the Thames River.

"We did work on regulatory issues at a time when England and Europe were way ahead of North America because of population density—a natural reason," Newell says. Warner predicted everything that would happen in North America and told the young Newell he could write his own ticket if he established himself as a credible environmental engineer. Newell struck out for the new world and has made his company a model not just in environmental protection and cleanup, but also in helping Natives benefit. Some 700 Natives work with Syncrude in various capacities. In one year, the company spent almost $100 million on Native businesses, nearly half the total of the whole industry.

"Syncrude was green when green was only a colour," says Newell. "In our industry we really do disturb the environment, but we know that. Even in the early 1970s, when we had to drain water off, a lot of care was taken in how to do that. But a proper spillway was put in. That cost $35 million in 1973, which gives an idea of the commitment.

"On the reclamation side, we always did reclaim as we went along. We step past the old MBA argument of pushing out costs as far as possible; instead we do it now, reclaiming as fast as we can."

Suncor, the other big oilsands operator, has worked hard in recent years to set new benchmarks for environmental and community performance. "Companies need to earn societal respect to grow their businesses," says Lambert. "As companies, we're never the owners of the resources we develop—the people of the province are. You need to engage the communities where you operate; you need to address issues and concerns proactively; and you need to achieve levels of environmental performance that meet or exceed stakeholder expectations."

All this, continues Lambert, is encompassed within the general concept of sustainability. Suncor is part of the Dow Jones Sustainability Index, which measures corporate performance by all three standards: social, environmental, and economic.

"As soon as you are able to demonstrate actual shareholder benefits to sustainability efforts," says Lambert, "everybody wakes up very quickly. It puts sustainability into the mainstream, as opposed to being something peripheral. In our case, it has helped us attract European investors. It's a big trend—the link of sustainability to shareholder value."

The Dow Jones Sustainability Index excludes companies that make alcohol, tobacco, firearms, or armaments, but includes firms from industries considered "traditionally polluting"—such as oil— if they "lead their industries toward more sustainability by setting standards for best practice and demonstrating superior environmental, social and economic performance."[16]

To Gwyn Morgan of EnCana Corp., his company's good reputation is not only a matter of honour; it's also a key element in success. "From the corporate viewpoint, your reputation is so important," Morgan says. "When we're telling a farmer we'd like to drill a well or build a pipeline on his property, I want our name to be such that he says, 'Oh yeah, okay, this is a company that's got a good reputation. I hear they've dealt fairly with other people; I hear they have a good track record.' That's the way we want to be thought of everywhere we work, both in the environment and in community investment."

When corporate leaders talk about "community investment," they mean the whole range of donations and contributions that companies make to everything from foundations to churches, schools, playgrounds, hockey teams, and much larger community projects. Some companies still take a passive approach by simply sifting through applications and choosing winners and losers. But the most responsible oil and gas companies now have top executives in charge of their programs, and they're serious about making corporate dollars count for the good of the community. Those new buzzwords, "community investment," are meant to show that the companies aren't simply trying to touch up their image (although that's certainly one goal). They're also trying to improve the world around them.

"It wasn't that long ago that the donations activity consisted of sending out cheques in response to myriad funding requests," says Hazel Gillespie, Petro-Canada's manager of national community investment. "We've gone well beyond that now to an era where we clearly realize that this isn't just about issuing cheques. It's about hands, hearts, and minds—getting involved and helping to address community issues and opportunities. It's about working together to form strong relationships to get done the things that need to be done. It's about being strategic to create business and community wins."[17]

Dick Wilson, EnCana's vice-president of public relations, has followed that credo for many years, tackling so many community projects that everyone who knows him has lost count.

"It simply makes for a better country," he says. "We can't be everything to everybody, so we focus on particular areas that relate to a better business and a better community. At EnCana they are health and wellness, youth, education and the environment, and capacity-building within a community. We say we give a hand up, not a handout."[18]

Much of EnCana's social activism comes from CEO Morgan, a thoughtful man who believes that a company without a social heart isn't worth much, and that communities need active companies to fully develop their potential.

"I think a successful business is the heart and soul of a successful country and a successful society," he says. "If you don't have successful businesses, you try to find me a country where the standard of living is good and the social programs even exist. Business has to be an extension of the community."

Nowhere is EnCana's commitment more obvious than in Ecuador, where the company is the largest foreign investor in the oil and gas industry, with nearly $2 billion at stake.

One of EnCana's two founding companies, Alberta Energy, bought the Ecuadorian interests from another Calgary firm, Pacalta, in 1999. Pacalta had already created the Nanpaz ("Road to Peace") Foundation, mainly to help the environment and people of the Ecuadorian Amazon, where poverty is rampant and clear-cutting of rainforests has been almost uncontrolled. Alberta

Energy expanded on Pacalta's commitments and continues today as EnCana, a still larger company formed in 2002 by the merger of Alberta Energy and PanCanadian Energy.

Executives who visit Ecuador are always touched by the plight of indigenous people and colonists in the region and are heartened that through their firm they can actually help. The company has built free health clinics and spends heavily on schools, community centres, and other social facilities. Even before EnCana was formed, Alberta Energy reported that "the company has spent US $8.7 million for roads, bridges, schools and other infrastructure projects in Sucumbios Province and other provinces of Amazonia." Through the Nanpaz Foundation, the company helped local residents establish "self-sufficient integral farms," which allow families to feed and care for themselves while selling their surpluses. About 28 such farms have been set up so far, and after the second year of operation, they return average monthly revenue of US $708 to the self-sufficient farmers. On top of all this, nearly 2,000 Ecuadorians work directly and indirectly for EnCana in jobs from senior manager to unskilled labourer.

Canadian Native leaders are also impressed by this ethic. Alberta Native leader Chief Joyce Metchewais, whose band at Cold Lake in Alberta has a business arrangement with EnCana, says the company actually asks questions of Natives, then listens to the answers. In the past, this tactic has been used to dupe Natives, she says, but the new goal is exactly the opposite. The company really wants to adapt and help, she said with wonder, after her band signed its deal.[19]

Barbara Zach, EnCana's vice-president of international relations, says the emphasis in other countries is always on helping people become self-sufficient. "We inherited the Nanpaz Foundation and we also have our community-relations program within the company," she says. "Within Ecuador, in both of those areas, we try to build the capacity. We want to ensure that the community is left better off than what it was."[20]

Some of the most useful expenditures are the small ones. The company bought a school bus for children who had to walk miles to classes. It helped schools start vegetable gardens so the kids could be fed at lunch. Nanpaz conducts training in vital skills, and the students then spread those skills around their communities. Indigenous people, who have lost much of their culture in a flood of colonization, get help in recovering old skills such as collecting plants for herbal remedies.

"Ecuador doesn't have a good history with the oil companies," says Zach, "but EnCana is showing that they are not all the same—oil companies can do good. How we operate in Alberta is how we operate internationally—we take those standards and community programs and modify them to suit what is appropriate in that country. We're always trying to find out what the best practices are and incorporate them into everything we do. We want to provide value and give back to the community."

EnCana is an exceptionally careful company when it operates abroad, for reasons that go far beyond altruism. Foreign operations are fraught with political and public relations dangers, especially for companies that ignore local politics and environments. Calgary's Talisman Energy has been hurt by international campaigns against its operations in Sudan, where oil revenues help an oppressive government stay in power. In 2001, Occidental Petroleum was threatened with a mass tribal suicide if it drilled on ancestral lands. Chevron Texaco was embarrassed in mid-2002 when Nigerian women demanding jobs for relatives occupied several oil installations. Shell's Nigerian operations have been a running scandal for many years, with major pollution problems and allegations that Shell backs government violence. The company was vilified in 1995 when the Nigerian regime hanged poet Ken Saro-Wiwa, along with eight other members of his Ogoni tribe, after they opposed Shell's operations on their lands. Shell also spawned huge international protests in 1996 when it wanted to dispose of its redundant Brent Spar floating oil platform by sinking it in the Atlantic Ocean. Greenpeace responded by occupying the platform several times and raised protests in the United Kingdom, Germany, and other countries. Shell backed down, but the public relations damage was enormous. Exxon suffered almost as much harm from its callous response to the *Exxon Valdez* oil spill off the coast of Alaska in 1989.

But there's another side even to that infamous story, told by Danish political scientist and statistician Bjorn Lomborg, a self-described "old left-wing Greenpeace member" who finds that many claims by environmentalists don't hold up under his "statistical microscope." In his fascinating book, *The Skeptical Environmentalist*, Lomborg says the *Exxon Valdez* accident "has become the symbol of the big greedy company that without consideration for the environment triggers an ecological catastrophe."[21] But his conclusion is "that although the immediate biological loss in Alaska was high, it was roughly the equivalent of one day of plate glass death to birds in the US or two days of domestic cat kill in Britain. Another thought-provoking comparison is that the overall pollution was less than 2 percent of pollution caused by powerboats in the US every year. And finally, that all actors agree that the Sound has almost fully recovered or will do so within decades."[22]

That doesn't excuse Exxon from its casual early response, or the industry from facing many serious questions. Today, it can be forced to answer very quickly because of a new factor—the Internet. Greenpeace used cyberspace to launch the Brent Spar protest and caught the company by surprise. From that moment it was evident that protestors no longer need to rely on the traditional media to organize rallies and actions and broadcast their message—they can do it all on the Internet at lightning speed. For companies that act and respond foolishly, the damage can be indelible. An Internet search of the words "Brent Spar" or "Shell" and "Nigeria" will still turn up hundreds of references. Photos of seabirds killed by the Exxon disaster linger on Web pages, reminding everyone of the dangers of spills and perpetuating the harm to Exxon nearly a decade and a half after the accident. Thousands of negative opinions about oil companies, some well-informed, others absolute nonsense, are instantly accessible to anyone with an Internet connection. Much of the criticism is propelled by an unshakeable conviction that fossil fuels should not be used for any purpose and must be phased out. One typical Web site, CorpWatch, concedes that natural gas is a clean fuel, then concludes: "Natural gas is at best an incremental improvement over oil, and at worst a distraction from the real challenge of moving our economies beyond fossil fuels."[23] There's no convincing critics who start from the belief that the industry has no right to exist.

In large measure, the industry's strategy is a response to this unrelenting and effective opposition. Companies hire public relations experts, set up their own Web sites, and launch advertising campaigns to show that they care about the environment. The best response—more common than the critics think—is the strengthened resolve of good companies to perform well, both environmentally and socially. There's no doubt that the Internet environmental movement, with its pursuit of issues both real and imagined, has forced the industry to perform better. Ironically, the very people who believe the oil and gas business should fold up its tent have helped make it more acceptable to the larger public.

In Canada, the industry is clearly winning new friends. An Ipsos-Reid poll in October 2001 showed that 56 per cent of Canadians believe the oil industry's environmental performance has improved in recent times.[24] The percentage is lowest in Ontario (49 per cent) and highest in all the producing provinces of the West and Atlantic Canada. The most telling result is in Alberta, where fully 80 per cent of respondents said the industry has improved. Nobody knows the business, with all its warts, better than Albertans, who live and work alongside thousands of oil wells, pipelines, and natural gas plants. Many Albertans employed in oil and gas or related industries are contemptuous of shoddy practices and are quick to say so. The reasons are both personal and environmental. "I get e-mails and letters from our employees about anything environmental they're concerned about," says Gwyn Morgan. "Of course they're concerned."

Still, the shift is far from universal in the industry. Some companies talk a good environmental and social game but don't play it. "Not all people get it, even at the CEO levels," says Syncrude's Eric Newell. "Small companies don't have the resource of people, so it's more difficult for them. You need the will, and someone has to be the catalyst. And you have to work hard at it."[25] Profit is such a powerful motive in the industry that if the CEO doesn't back strong environmental action, a company will produce rhetoric but not much else. Martha Kostuch, a respected environmentalist and rural veterinarian who has poked and prodded the Alberta industry for 25 years, says, "The bottom line is that we've made some improvements, but still have a long way to go. One problem is the significant increase in the number of companies as well as the increase in activity. . . . While most companies are doing more to address environmental problems, the number of conflicts have still increased."[26]

Environmental consultant Barry Worbets, who has won awards for his environmental work with major oil companies, says, "There are some boards of directors who tell company environmentalists that they're paying too much attention to the environmental and sustainability issue."[27] Worbets knows that good corporate environmental experts have to be ready to fight such pressure, sometimes by putting their jobs on the line. Elaine McCoy, a former Alberta cabinet minister and president of the McLeod Institute for Environmental Analysis at the University of Calgary, knows that too many companies are laggard. "There are still some who say, 'If I put this [environmental] spin on it, my shareholders won't be nervous that I'm suddenly going to be blindsided.' A lot haven't caught on to this yet. The only thing still driving them is share-holder value."[28] These are the companies that believe in wind power—but only the kind that comes from their own lips. They hurt the whole industry and give credence to radical critics who say that all the industry's initiatives are just talk.

Yet even the toughest of the fair and responsible critics concede that huge gains have been made by many companies. Kostuch, for instance, believes that oil and gas should be phased out as soon as possible, but in the meantime she considers it her duty to help the companies improve. Like many environmentalists who actually achieve results, she will fight the oil companies if she thinks she must, but is equally ready to cooperate when the circumstances seem right. "Certainly I've seen enormous changes since I got involved nearly 25 years ago," Kostuch says. "Most have been positive. Companies in general are more receptive in recognizing the importance of environment and in addressing environmental concerns."

Tom Marr-Laing is director of Energy Watch for Alberta's Pembina Institute for Appropriate Development, a not-for-profit environmental policy and research organization. Marr-Laing acknowledges that his institute can be tough on the industry but he shares Kostuch's view of the attitude shift. "It would be totally off base to say that nothing has been done in five years and those guys are a bunch of yahoos," he says. "There are quite a number of people working within the industry who understand the issues and are progressive. . . . They are often a joy to work with." The changes were propelled by public pressure, he feels. "There was an oil-field crisis of confidence. We reached a point where there was a gap between where the public expected industry to operate and where government and industry were actually at." He adds that the industry still offers "the full spectrum from dinosaurs to advanced mammals . . . but over the past five or six years, there has been a shifting from pure dinosaur approach."[29]

The Royal Dutch/Shell Group of Companies, thought of as a typical dinosaur only a few years ago, is today in the midst of a remarkable turnaround in its corporate units in Europe, the United States, and Canada. One sign: Royal Dutch/Shell is the leading company in the energy section of the Dow Jones Sustainability Index. The U.S. division of the company, rather than focusing on profits, trumpets community achievements like an award from the Houston Food Bank. In May 2002, Shell Canada published its 11th annual *Sustainable Development Report* to measure the company's performance against its goals.

"Shell Canada's vision is to be a leader in providing our products and services in a profitable and environmentally and socially responsible manner," says Tim Faithfull, president and chief executive officer. "To continually improve, we must be willing to regularly assess our efforts and publicly report on our performance."[30] The company noted that in the previous year it reduced greenhouse-gas emissions by 1 per cent, improved refinery efficiency by 2 per cent, invested $5.8 million in various community programs, and expanded Aboriginal business capacity, thus yielding a $25-million increase in local revenues.

Elaine McCoy believes Shell's transformation is genuine. "Shell was caught in Nigeria, and that was a major turning point for the company," she says. "The company asked itself what it had to do to earn the right to continue producing. . . . They did it out of enlightened self-interest. In Alberta, Shell is committed to the ecosystems they're operating in, and they are among the leaders in using low-impact seismic technology."

Like many oil companies, Shell doesn't concede that greenhouse gases cause global warming, but neither does it ignore the issue. "We start from the premise that we accept greenhouse gas is a significant issue," says Ray Woods, Shell Canada's senior operating officer for resources. "We believe that prudent precautionary measures should be taken to reduce greenhouse-gas emissions."

After detailing Shell's environmental and social policies, he says, "There's no doubt that a company whose attitude hasn't changed would be crazy."[31]

Most aren't crazy, or suicidal. The oilpatch is run by people who want the company to be around after fossil fuels run out or are phased out, producing some other kind of energy. So they're moving, some haltingly, some briskly, toward a new role in society. "The corporate social responsibility of a company means moving beyond the traditional bottom line to triple bottom line," says Elaine McCoy. "This isn't spin. It has ultimate value, and it's real."

From his perspective within the industry, David Pryce has watched the growth of environmental and social awareness for 20 years. "Literally hundreds of people are employed by the companies to resolve environmental and landowner issues," he says. "These people are professionals and scientists who work to find a proper balance between the environmental, social, and economic considerations." Some have been at it for so long, in fact, that they're on the verge of retiring from successful careers as environmental managers.

Oilman and financier Murray Edwards says, "The biggest change is that everybody today, whether in oil or gas or otherwise, is sensitive to the environment where they live. That sensitivity causes people to become more vigilant about conducting their business in an environmentally sound way. The companies are quite aware of managing environmental risk and can do it through being proactive. The big companies recognize that they have an obligation to all the stakeholders, and the environment is one of their stakeholders."[32]

The buck stops at the board of directors, and today's best boards ensure that environmental standards are constantly upgraded and upheld. For many of these people, the most frustrating thing of all is the public's dim awareness of their achievements, and the constant negative stereotyping of the industry.

The Outlaw

Whatever else Wiebo Ludwig might be, he is not a typical farmer from northern Alberta. Rural people in the Peace River area, where Ludwig lived when he committed his criminal acts against oil and gas installations, are stoical, modest, and tolerant of social, racial, and ethnic differences. They're always ready to help, and they love community gatherings, but they don't push themselves on their neighbours. Men and women earn respect through their hard work and honesty. Farm women often enjoyed equal status with men for much of the 20th century, in part because their work is indispensable to family and business. The region is a melting pot of English, French, Aboriginals, Metis, Americans, Chinese, Norwegians, and many other European settlers. Place names like Beaverlodge, Valhalla, LaGlace, and Elmworth reflect the diversity. There have been ethnic tensions—the Ku Klux Klan had a mercifully brief run in the 1930s—but in the main, the people of the Peace let each other live in peace. The social fabric is loose but tough, like the comfortable webbing of an old summer hammock.[1]

Eccentrics and strong women have always found their place. During the Depression, the great sociologist C.A. Dawson was fascinated by a Mrs. Edwards, who still took cattle to the range near

Pouce Coupe, at age 70. Shocked, he observed that Mrs. Edwards was "a bit rough and swears."[2] (Pouce Coupe is just on the B.C. side of the Alberta border, a few kilometres south of Dawson Creek.) A certain Mrs. Hart owned the hotel at Pouce Coupe, built the verandah herself, and had "a superb business sense."[3] This was a land of survival economics, where a half-dead horse, useful as mink feed, could be traded for 100 pounds of sugar.[4] Dawson found that the population included "a great many freaks" and "many others who are queer and unadjusted."[5] Among them were the doctor who might or might not have had a medical education, the peculiar dentist-homesteader, and a whole series of independent women who failed to fit Dawson's lingering Victorian stereotypes.[6]

He could have been describing the odd ducks who migrate to any frontier, but Dawson and others also noted in this evolving Peace River society great kindness, tolerance, generosity, and cooperation. Family life was close and warm, marked by skating parties in winter and picnics in summer.[7] On great occasions like community gatherings or sports competitions, families would decamp and travel for a whole day, sometimes taking the cows along with them.[8] Children grew up to be independent and resourceful. The ones who went to high school—not many in those early days—had to board in a town. Although this early society has changed vastly because modern transportation and economics have scattered many families off the farm, the essential strictures remain: Work hard; help your neighbour; settle boundary disputes peacefully; respect differences where you can and ignore them where you can't.

Ludwig and his clan at Trickle Creek are certainly eccentric, and many call them queer and unadjusted, but otherwise they are atypical of both the Peace Country's history and its values. Intolerant of any beliefs but their own, they preach the subservience of women to men, to the point of shaving heads for disobedience.[9]

They keep their children out of the school system and require strict obedience to the patriarch. "Public education is an abomina-

tion," Ludwig told a writer for *Outside Magazine*, an American publication.[10] "I would rather see my children dead than be taken to
school." Ludwig loves such talk and enjoys situations where people have to listen to his pronouncements. After he was charged, he
said he was thinking about running for the leadership of Alberta's
Social Credit Party, a now moribund outfit that has been a haven
for intolerant misfits on the extreme right.

Despite all this, the tolerant locals would have accepted the
Ludwigs if it weren't for other qualities that farmers found deeply
offensive. The clan claimed to be self-sufficient on marginal land
that every farmer knew couldn't possibly support such a large
group. "They don't raise enough stuff to live themselves," says
neighbour Rob Everton. "I don't know of a farm in this area that
could support nearly 40 people."[11] Neighbour Dymphny Dronyk
caught a telling contradiction in the clan's pride in the food they
say comes from the farm. "All they say is, 'The land is poisoned,
the land is poisoned, the land is poisoned.' Then they offer you
what they say is organic honey or butter from the land. And I say,
'How is that honey not poisoned? How is that butter not poisoned?' Why does no one pick up on that?"[12]

Ludwig's love of a high podium and undivided attention, especially from the media, came to annoy many of his neighbours.
During his trial, after dominating media coverage for days with his
speeches outside the courtroom, Ludwig could hardly bear to see
reporters turn to his neighbour Rob Everton for another take on
the story. He began to heckle Everton and only shut up when a
young TV reporter told him it was finally someone else's turn.[13]

My first experience with Ludwig was typical for those who con-
tradict him: Ludwig grabbed my arm and shouted at me when I
asked him questions he didn't like.[14]

Dymphny Dronyk, who worked in the community for Alberta
Energy Company (AEC), endured this kind of treatment for many
months. Living near the Ludwig clan, she was subjected to his

harangues about her status as a single parent and her need for a man to make decisions for her. Members of the group first deluged her with environmental polemics and offers of babysitting. She was offended by the implication that as a woman she couldn't look after herself. When she finally managed to make her lack of interest clear, the tactics changed from wooing to what she feels was bullying. The tires on her truck were flattened 11 times by nails. Ludwig once came to her home, walked in, dropped money on the table, and stood so close that his belly touched hers. Dronyk courageously stared him down.[15] She feels that the whole game was designed to coerce her to join the clan. "In a nutshell, they wanted me and my kids. I'm young. I'm Dutch. I like kids. We're good breeding stock.

"It was so demeaning. They just had this quiet way of somehow making you feel you were wrong, you were somehow bad. There were so many days when I just wanted to run and never come back. But I am Dutch and I'm stubborn—there's no way he's going to push me around. I knew I might be doing a dangerous thing when I spoke to Christie Blatchford [of the *National Post*]," she says. "But after the article came out, it was a catalyst. People in the community were wonderful and supportive. They didn't know I was going through all that."[16]

If there was dissent among the 40 or so daughters, sons, wives, children, and other acolytes at Trickle Creek, it didn't reach the outside world. "It is Wiebo's thoughts, Wiebo's sentence structure, Wiebo's view of the planet that you hear," wrote Christie Blatchford, one of the few journalists who realized that Ludwig is more authoritarian cult leader than ecological hero. I vividly recall Ludwig's wife, Mamie, trembling as he harangued me, yet supporting his every utterance like a bedraggled parrot.

The bizarre thing about the Ludwig saga is how much had to be ignored in order to turn him into an ecological icon—his paternalism, his far-right ideology, his conviction that outsiders are hell-bound—all the things that liberals and leftists are supposed to deplore. Yet as big-city reporters flooded in and chowed down at his Trickle Creek compound, many were blinkered to anything beyond the compelling notion of the virtuous subsistence farmers fighting against evil Big Oil. Bombing, shooting, and sabotage were excused away, even though Ludwig never completely denied them, because his unproven charges about the industry had such a fine ring to them. "The Ludwigs are extremely persuasive and they played the media like a fine instrument," says Rob Everton, who started a petition circulated among Ludwig's near neighbours. Forty-two signed the document, swearing that they'd experienced nothing like the health and environmental problems that Ludwig insisted were plaguing his clan. "Our story was not sensational; it didn't grab headlines," Everton adds. "Everyone likes to see someone confrontational, not ordinary people making a living. That's not newsworthy. We were untrained; we didn't have the knack for the sound bites that made the national news." One outcome for many local people was a complete loss of faith in the media. "I now wonder what's really going on whenever I look at TV and read the paper," says Dronyk. "I question everything. I know now that it's our responsibility to find out what's going on, rather than spout off a headline."[17]

Everton, a perceptive man, figures that Ludwig managed to tap into the urbanite's longing for a simple rural life. "Wiebo Ludwig became a rural myth and he promoted it," says Everton. "He wasn't living it as much as he portrayed it. You could hardly walk into McDonald's in Grande Prairie and not find someone from his clan sitting there." Ludwig also appealed to environmentalists who liked the idea of a self-sufficient man fighting an industry that shouldn't exist because it exploits fossil fuels. Media credulity over the Ludwigs' medical and scientific claims could be astonishing. *Outside Magazine* accepted without comment the clan's belief that a baby, the child of Wiebo's son Bo and daughter-in-law

Renée, was stillborn and deformed because of exposure to sour gas. Yet two pages earlier the reporter notes that the Ludwigs "treat everything from diaper rash to whooping cough with extracts from their herb garden." The clan shuns medical treatment and no autopsy was ever performed on the baby. They have no evidence that sour gas caused the sad stillbirth. When the *National Post*'s Blatchford pointed this out to Mamie Ludwig, her response was "Proof! You people always want proof! We know! We don't need proof!"[18]

The most bizarre part of the Ludwig saga, odder even than the bombings, is the loss of this child, named Abel Ryan Ludwig, in August 1998. It became tangled in dangerous symbolism with the bombings and shooting death of local teenager Karman Willis on the Ludwig property nearly a year later. Nobody doubts the sincere grief the clan must have felt at their child's stillbirth, but the reaction shows Wiebo's penchant for crashing through boundaries of behaviour. Before burying the remains in a wooden box on the farm, the clan made a five-minute video showing the parents caressing and stroking the malformed child, and sent the cassette to Alberta Energy Company. Everyone who has seen the video finds it strange and difficult viewing. The death also prompted Ludwig to make his single most inflammatory comment: "Abel Ryan was killed by the polluters. Sometimes I think we should take the president of Alberta Energy Company hostage, tie him up, make him watch the video of Abel Ryan, and then slit his throat."[19] Ludwig, who later claimed this was a joke, was never called to account for what seemed to be a clear death threat against an individual, Gwyn Morgan, the CEO of Alberta Energy.

By the time the child was born dead, the Peace country was riven with tension over the Ludwigs' rhetoric and the oilpatch sabotage. In December 1997 fire broke out in a Norcen Energy well. Shotgun shells were found encased in cement at the site—a potentially deadly booby trap. A few months later, shots were fired at an

Alberta Energy well site, and on June 16 a projectile bomb hit an AEC pipeline. Suncor was also hit, as was Union Pacific. Ruptured lines twice released deadly hydrogen sulphide gas, forcing evacuations and road closures. On August 24, 1998, three days after the stillbirth, a bomb went off at a Suncor well near Hinton, 200 kilometres from the Ludwig farm. Ludwig, his son Bo, and Richard Boonstra, Renée's father, were arrested at a roadblock near the site. Ludwig had explosive residue on his hands and was dressed in camouflage gear, but a few weeks later, charges were dropped for lack of evidence.

The sabotage struck many companies over a wide area, but the suspicion always came back to the Ludwig clan. Their wild talk invited it. Ludwig made these typical statements, among others, to me: "Sometimes, to reflect verbal perseverance, some force has to be exercised. I'm supportive of it." He suggested that more would happen and "it's no game. It will make bombing look minor. . . . I'm somewhat aware of the people who are doing it, who are angry."[20] Earlier, the sympathetic *Outside Magazine* had elicited even more inflammatory words from Ludwig: "Well, you have to love your enemy enough to win him over through persuasion rather than kill him. But if he needs to be killed to restrain his madness, then you kill him. That's not murder. It's executing judgment." Ludwig is a master at hinting at responsibility without quite confessing it. To Christie Blatchford he said, "Your words are more dangerous than my dynamite," then added quickly, "my verbal dynamite."

Ludwig's neighbours were appalled and frightened by the sabotage and the escalating rhetoric. "The Ludwigs have said they condone the sour gas bombings," says Rob Everton. "I have a real problem with that. When you're arguing against the dangers of hydrogen sulphide—and nobody disputes that—the last thing you do is condone blowing up facilities and allowing it to be emitted uncontrolled in the atmosphere."

Brian Peterson, who formed the West County Concerned Citizens group to help keep the area calm, was offended by yet another double standard. "Those bombs had a huge impact on people," he says. "If they had been exploding in Edmonton or Calgary, we'd have had the military out here. There was probably less bombing during the FLQ crisis. But it was out here in the hinterland, so this was a great place to fit into the political agenda."[21]

Most victim companies responded to the assaults by beefing up security and quietly helping their frightened employees cope. Only one, Alberta Energy, took a critical extra step and decided to deal with Ludwig. Gwyn Morgan, the man Ludwig threatened to kidnap and kill, even agreed to meet him personally. Morgan now feels that any attempt at conciliation with Wiebo Ludwig is certain to fail.

"There was a promise that came directly that if I would simply agree to meet with him, our people would be able to have a safe Christmas," Morgan says. "Our employees were very anxious; they were just terrified." Morgan thought he might find common ground with Ludwig, but now says, "It was pretty obvious that was impossible. . . . But once he got me engaged, then he had something. He needed to engage one of the senior guys. Some companies had more incidents than we had, but they didn't get engaged. Once that happened, then there was a whole different agenda there."[22]

Part of Ludwig's agenda was to sell his property to AEC. He first offered it for $1.25 million, then upped his price to $1.5 million, and finally backed down to $1.325 million. During the negotiation, one AEC site was bombed and another shot at. The curious timing was part of the reason for extortion charges against Ludwig, but later they would be thrown out during his trial by Justice Sterling Sanderman. The judge ruled that not only was there no evidence against Ludwig, but also no evidence that AEC had been induced to bargain with him.

The company clearly wanted a deal with Ludwig, and by mid-July 1998, the parties seemed to have one. AEC would buy the land for $800,000, nearly twice its value. But Ludwig balked at a late AEC condition: He and his clan would have to agree never to live within 800 kilometres of the site. The company's reasoning was obvious: If the Ludwigs were the bombers, they could simply use AEC's money to buy a better farm and continue their sabotage. There's little doubt, however, that the clause carried a whiff of desperation and might even have been in violation of the Canadian constitution. In any case, Ludwig backed out at the end of July. Over the August long weekend, two well sites were blown up by persons unknown. Ludwig later tried to re-open negotiations, perhaps realizing that he'd chased the golden goose back to Calgary forever. But Abel Ryan Ludwig was born dead only days later, and any chance of reconciliation vanished. For a community already in shock, there was still plenty of trouble to come.

Is Ludwig right about sour gas poisoning the land, water, and air, causing animal death and deformities, and even human stillbirth? He has no hard evidence, but the assumption that he is correct drives much of the sympathy for the clan. Many Albertans could appreciate his chagrin at having as many as 10 wells ring his property when none had been there when he bought it. He found himself caught in a typical conundrum of oil and gas country: Those who own mineral rights have as much claim in law to enjoy the benefits as the residents who buy land with surface rights. This creates a built-in conflict, especially when the landowner makes his home on the property and the oil companies arrive with their noisy trucks and drilling rigs (and payments for the farmer, too). The health question has simmered in rural areas for decades, with many farmers convinced that sour gas, even in small concentrations, affects the health of cattle and humans. This is a reasonable suspicion for the obvious reason that hydrogen sulphide is deadly poison that has killed oilfield workers. Leaks and blowouts can be lethal, and every responsible company has emergency plans to deal with them. In 1994, farmer Wayne Johnson complained that a leak near Sundre, Alberta, sickened and killed some of his cattle. An Alberta Agriculture study later confirmed that the leak had indeed affected the health of the animals.[23] The conclusion was hardly surprising: High concentrations of the gas are extremely dangerous.

Even when there's no danger, another intangible can affect rural residents: Sour gas smells awful, and even small doses of it can spoil a person's enjoyment of the family home. This alone alienates and enrages some farmers and ranchers. Adding to their bitterness is the suspicion, probably true, that city-dwellers would never have to tolerate such noxious odours—although they are sometimes treated to an appalling whiff. Few people who lived in central Alberta in 1982 will forget the sickening odour of the biggest release of sour gas ever in Canada, the Lodgepole well blowout that took 68 days to cap and spread gas over a 400-kilometre radius that included Edmonton.

But leaks and blowouts are industrial accidents, not frequent occurrences. The industry has been working hard to reduce both venting—the planned release of small amounts of "sweet," or non-sour, natural gas—and flaring. Sour gas, however, is never released intentionally. The Canadian industry's safety record is high by international standards and still improving. As a result, many Western farmers and urban residents live near wells and gas plants for their whole lives without being subjected to accidents or even odours. Studies have failed to prove a health risk to animals or humans from exposure to gas at the levels found on farms during routine operations. (See Chapter Six for a full analysis.)

Nonetheless, Ludwig hit the nerve of all the suspicions and fears with his unrestrained allegations. He claimed at various times that leaks from sour wells around his farm caused animal miscarriages;

birth defects; skin problems; chronic respiratory illnesses; memory loss; eye and throat infections; the death of 60 animals, including lambs, goats, and cows; and, of course, the stillbirth of baby Abel. His notes on the subject run to hundreds of pages. He has filed many complaints, focusing first on disruption of the family's plans for a quiet Christian life unimpeded by industrialization, and then, increasingly, on health problems. A Grande Prairie field office of the Energy and Utilities Board (EUB) has recorded well over 100 communications with Ludwig over the years.[24] The most vivid came on January 2, 1997, when he spilled crude oil in the agency's office, ostensibly to give regulators a bitter whiff of the odours he says his family endures.

Yet the Ludwigs seem to have little interest in establishing scientific credibility for their claims. As Mamie said, they just know, and believe their deep conviction should be enough to convince others. According to Gwyn Morgan and the EUB's Greg Gilbertson, the Ludwigs rejected an offer of a fully independent study to get to the bottom of any health problems on the farm.

"We said to him [Ludwig], 'Okay, you take charge of engaging, say, the University of Calgary faculty of environmental design,'" says Morgan. "We said, 'You engage them to take every soil sample and examine all of the issues and come up with an independent report, and we will provide the money to pay for it. You will be in charge of the report and we will have nothing to say about the report.' We didn't dictate who it would be, except that it would have to be somebody credible.

"At the meeting, he suggested he would think about that. Of course, he turned that down. He had to turn that down because, I think, there were lots of things he didn't want people to talk about."

Morgan says one reason he decided to deal with Ludwig was his concern that the industry might actually bear some responsibility for any health problems on the farm. "One of the fundamental things, from the industry point of view, was how we could figure out what was wrong, what was causing these alleged problems. And there are some real problems—miscarriages and things like that."

Most farmers know that other factors, including lack of the mineral selenium in the soil, can cause birthing problems in animals. Morgan recalls: "When I was on the farm, we had to provide our cattle with a salt lick that had selenium and a few other things in it. The people who didn't use it had [animal] miscarriage problems and it was well known in the industry."

Rob Everton says the region of Ludwig's farm has precisely that problem. "We're definitely deficient in selenium. This started showing up in the 1960s and '70s. If he isn't doing that, he's heading for big trouble. You need these supplements for the cattle. My theory is that he's not up to date. I personally think it's a nutrition problem there. . . . He's an organic farmer and lots of these people don't believe in supplements of any kind. He's certainly not the kind of man to take advice from agricultural experts or vets."

The most damaging counter to Ludwig's case is that many farmers live in the same immediate area but experience none of the problems he complains about. The Evertons' 42 signatures on their petition are the clearest proof of this. All these people flatly state that the industry is not affecting the health of their families and animals, or poisoning their environment. Nonetheless, some critics imply that their testimony is tainted because the industry holds them in thrall with jobs or payments for use of their land. This assumption that only the Ludwigs are right, and all the others are either too foolish to see the truth or too venal to acknowledge it, is an insult to decent people who are every bit as concerned about the health of their families as Ludwig is.

"We felt upset that Wiebo Ludwig was taken as speaking for the community," says Gisela Everton, Rob's wife. "We wrote that letter saying we have not had any of the same kind of problems, and we took that letter around to our neighbours and those 42 people signed it. None of them had the problems that Wiebo Ludwig had. We didn't find anybody who was complaining of the same things—nobody, not one single person.

"For the most part, the oil companies are trying their best to do things and run their operations the best way possible. They're not out there to poison the environment. Some companies are better than others, but they have a commodity that all of us need and are making improvements all the time, like reducing flaring. These are good things to be doing."[25]

Rob Everton adds, "Certainly no one is experiencing the massive wreck these guys are claiming. The cow-calf people here are making a very good living, although they have to be very productive and there's lots of hard work. If you start to get into 2 to 3 per cent death-loss, you have a problem. This year [2002] has been really tough because of the bad weather, but they are experiencing great success with good management."

Everton feels that when Ludwig first started having problems in the early 1990s, "he happened to clash with some dinosaurs and he went ballistic. There are still some dinosaurs out there and I've personally run into them and they can be the most unpleasant people to deal with. But usually it doesn't take more than a phone call or two. You bypass the dinosaur and you get things sorted out. . . . I think Wiebo Ludwig needs a scapegoat to maintain that control. He doesn't want to be seen as making mistakes of his own. He can't be challenged."

Many people were deeply offended that Ludwig's claims portrayed the whole area as polluted, dangerous, and even barely habitable. Brian Peterson has been frustrated by this for years. "They get all the rhetoric in the media," he says. "To have something portrayed one way, and for it to be totally different behind the scenes, that's hard to live with. I've dealt with reporters from Toronto who just had no idea. . . . I felt that the media started out with an environmental hero in their minds and had a hard time shaking that. They created it—you could tell by the direction of the stories and where they were going."

The Evertons live just over a mile from the Ludwigs and seldom catch even a whiff of sour gas. This is typical in the area: The unwelcome odour is rarely detected, and when it is, everybody treats it as an emergency. "Just a tiny whiff, that means something is vastly wrong," says Rob Everton.[26] "A while ago I smelled one hint of sour gas—I was probably two to three hundred metres away from a well. That was at ten at night. I called the company's emergency number and within half an hour there were people there. There was a small leak and they fixed it right away. That's how it's supposed to work, and if it doesn't somebody at the company's in serious trouble." The Evertons are skeptical of the Ludwigs' implication that the family suffers constantly from noxious odours. "I don't know how, if it was that bad, we couldn't smell it and they could," says Everton. "They like to claim all the toxic gases funnel into their little world. I have a tough time with that one."

Everton freely admits that the wells themselves can be "a pain in the neck. There are hundreds of them around here. They stick them in the middle of your field and you've got to work around them. They're an inconvenience. But I also realize that we need those products in everyday life." The companies pay about $10,000 to the farmer when they drill a well, and another $2,000 a year while the well operates. For many, these payments are a significant part of farm revenue.

The Evertons have only one well on their land, which pays them $2,200 annually. When they step out of their house, they don't see a single well anywhere in their wide field of view. That's hardly unique for local farmers. "It's a good life, and the air quality in this area is as good as or better than anywhere else in the province," Everton says.

He's right, according to a study released May 23, 2002. Alberta's Health and Wellness Department, in cooperation with the

Mistahia Health Region, completed a two-year study of air quality in the Grande Prairie area. The reason for the study, the government euphemistically said, was to answer questions from area residents "regarding air quality in view of ongoing oil, gas and other industrial activity in the area."[27] The more direct reason was Wiebo Ludwig. For 28 weeks, 130 volunteers provided urine and blood samples, submitted lifestyle and health information, and wore "a series of circular monitors designed to capture a variety of airborne contaminants." Each volunteer participated for a week, keeping a careful diary of daily activities.

The study concluded that levels of major air pollutants, including sulphur dioxide, the byproduct of sour gas flaring, exist in the Grande Prairie area at levels well below Alberta's ambient air quality guidelines. One group, volatile organic compounds from gasoline, solvents, and other products, was more concentrated in people's homes than in the air outside. Local air quality, in other words, has less to do with air pollution than with how people handle chemicals in the home. "Particulate matter was also measured at levels lower than proposed Canada wide standards," the study concluded.[28] Alberta Health and Wellness stated flatly that the study "confirms Grande Prairie area residents are breathing good quality air and suffer less respiratory illnesses than experienced in other communities in Alberta. . . . No other significant differences were found in the health of Grande Prairie residents. Rates of illness, disease, chronic conditions, lung function, neurocognitive function, as well as exposure to contaminants were similar to other communities across the province." This is a direct scientific contradiction of anecdotal claims, widely circulated in publications like *Outside Magazine*, that area residents suffer high levels of cancer and other diseases allegedly caused by the oil and gas industry.

Although the night of June 20, 1999, was one of lingering northern twilight, most residents of the Peace country remember it as the darkest in living memory. All the fear and anger sown in the community mixed spontaneously with teenage bravado, and the lethal combustion killed a teenage girl. The news spread across Canada like a prairie fire—somebody had shot Karman Willis, 16, while she was joyriding on the Ludwig property with seven male friends. The last ride the girl would ever take was one she'd never wanted to join.

Flying at the front of the Ludwig farm was a black flag flaunting a skull and crossbones. Local teens had long wanted to seize that flag, but they had no idea they would help make it a toxic symbol of the bitter relations between the compound and the community.

Karman Willis was a reluctant passenger in the truck that took her to her death. She decided to remain with her boyfriend, Brian Petterson, in his Chevy Supercab, along with three other friends. Petterson joined up with Dustin Dueck and the two trucks headed down the highway looking for fun. It was the summer solstice, when even at midnight an enterprising fellow could sit out in the twilight and read the *Grande Prairie Herald Tribune*.[29]

By four a.m., their target was in sight. The two trucks roared onto the Ludwig property, drove around, and rushed off. As they sped away, shots were fired and a bullet hit Karman Willis in the chest.

Ludwig told me later that one of the trucks was heading toward a tent where four of the Ludwig young women were sleeping. "The girls [ages 20, 18, 16, and 9] were terrified. The trucks were backfiring and it sounded like shots. The young kids in the truck were drunk and throwing beer cans. I thought it was thunder at first and then I realized it was something else. I rushed out to the door in my underwear. They were just driving out the gate at that point."[30]

Ludwig said he had no way of knowing who fired the shots and insisted that "they could have been shooting at us." While he said he was sad about Willis's death, he was quick to blame the parents, the police, and the oilpatch.

"Why are these kids out at that time? Parents bear responsibility for that kind of behaviour and shedding of blood. The police have stoked the kids up to give them the liberty to do that. I'm surprised the police haven't charged them. There are clear violations of the law. I feel bad for the parents. They have some serious pain. They should think a little bit from where it stems from."

Gisela Everton, Ludwig's neighbour, knows the teens shouldn't have been at the Ludwigs. "These were kids out partying, and someone had the bright idea that they'd steal the pirate flag featured prominently on the farm, right at the entrance to the property. Most of us would call the RCMP if kids were tearing around on our property. We wouldn't be shooting at them. It's true that these kids shouldn't have been there, but that doesn't excuse shooting at people. That crime of prankster doesn't rank someone being killed. The RCMP should have been called."[31]

The reactions around the country showed how divided Canadians were over the Ludwig saga. Most area residents were enraged that events had skidded fatally out of control. They knew the teens shouldn't have gone joyriding on the Ludwig farm—even the boys' parents admitted it freely—but they were appalled that somebody on the farm would shoot at trucks that were already on their way off the property. Brian Peterson summed up the sentiment when he said, "It was a cowardly act to shoot at these kids when they were leaving. If you see a bear, even if you're scared you don't shoot it as it runs away."

In Calgary, Alberta Energy CEO Gwyn Morgan was sickened by the news, and thought how sad it was that negotiations to buy the Ludwig property had fallen through. "It was a strange thing for us to be doing, thinking of buying their property. But we decided to pursue their offer and try to buy them out because we felt that if things kept blowing up, somebody was going to be killed. It could have been one of our employees or it could have been someone in the community. None of us ever dreamed it would be a young girl."

Ludwig, with his uncanny knack for pushing emotional buttons, continued to focus on the transgressions of the kids. They brought the tragedy on themselves by staying out late and drinking, he said.[32] He also blamed parents who don't control their children. "Whoever played a role in stoking up the reckless teens were clearly liable for Karman's murder," he said. "So the townspeople got themselves a huge spanking and a very painful one and a sad one, but I know that spankings can work some good in good time. That's my hope."

Ludwig also said, "They [parents] have to reflect on the part they played in it. It's a travesty of human behaviour to allow a 16-year-old out at four a.m. doing things like this to other people's lives."[33] The central fact that one of the intruders had lost her life seemed to strike in him no spark of empathy. His occasional reference to Karman's death being "sad" was only a backdrop to his moral thunder.

By this time the community was at a dangerous boiling point. Most felt that while the young people had made a mistake, Ludwig's preaching about Karman's death was almost unbearable. Ludwig was a man already charged with criminal offences in the bombings, who refused to condemn these illegal acts and hinted time and again that he was responsible for sabotage. He had talked openly about kidnapping a CEO and slitting his throat. He refused to renounce what he considered to be justified violence, yet claimed that any RCMP investigation of his actions was persecution. He seemed ill-placed to moralize about an episode of teenage trespassing that ended in death or to tell the community that it deserved a spanking. "Some of the things he said after Karman was killed were ridiculous," says Brian Peterson. "People were already on edge and riled up because of the bombings. That was like opening a huge wound and then pouring salt on it."

Amazingly, though, Ludwig's approach did win him sympathy, mainly from other parts of Canada. Even Karman Willis's parents received threats. Many calls and letters of support poured in to the clan. Ludwig had struck a chord with his complaints about wild teenagers invading someone else's property, a fear shared by many city-dwellers. Behind all this lay the assumption that Ludwig was some lonely hero fighting an evil industry and defending his virtuous homestead against marauding local rednecks. Much of his backing came from the environmental left—a strange twist, since it's hard to imagine anybody more red-necked than Wiebo Ludwig.

More than three years after Karman's death, the pain in the community is still powerful. "If any of the kids could change anything, they'd certainly take back that night," says Tahnis Petterson, mother of Karman's boyfriend, Brian Petterson (no relation to Brian Peterson).[34] "They have all been very remorseful. . . . I felt awful and a little responsible in a way—a girl lost her life. So does my son feel responsible. He knows he shouldn't have had Karman out there."

And Rob Everton makes a telling point about trespassing. "Wiebo Ludwig always says, 'Why aren't they being charged with trespassing?' Well, they as the property owners have never laid the charges. If they did that, they would be called upon to testify about the incident and then would have to tell the truth about what happened that night."

Much of what occurred later was not pleasant. Members of the Ludwig clan were denied service at stores in Hythe and other communities. Some were insulted and threatened with shooting and death. Karman Willis's older brother, Derek, beat up a Ludwig in-law in the mistaken belief he was one of Ludwig's sons.

The community's mood did not improve as the investigation into the shooting petered out with no results. The only charge the RCMP ever laid as a result of Karman's death—that of breaching bail conditions by having weapons on the farm—was dismissed by a judge as spurious.

And yet, despite all the fury, not much came of the threats against the Ludwigs in the Peace country. The community is peaceful at heart, much like any other in Canada, and before long its leaders were focused on healing rather than revenge. Brian Peterson and others formed West County Concerned Citizens, wanting to keep people level. They met the Ludwigs, hoping for reconciliation, but the talks, like many others with Ludwig, broke down. Peterson implies that Ludwig sabotaged any chance for understanding when the group began "getting through" to his boys, convincing them that nobody disapproved of them until they started their radical activities. But Ludwig wasn't the group's only focus or goal, Peterson says. "We formed it to bring the community back to the peacefulness that we had before." The group placed a sign that said "Remember Karman" on the Evertons' property—an act that some critics, inexplicably, see as hostile to the Ludwigs.

Karman's sad funeral service also revealed the essentially peaceful, forgiving nature of the community. Nearly a dozen people spoke, including several friends of the dead girl, and not one of them uttered a public word of intolerance or hostility toward the Ludwig clan. Indeed, they weren't mentioned at all, although the Reverend Chris Donnelly, who officiated, had a lot to say about choices. "Karman has paid a terrible price for a choice she has made," he said. "The young men who made the same choice will have to live with that choice for the rest of their lives. The family will also have to deal with the results of this choice for a long time."[36] By this point the audience was surely wondering about the Ludwigs' choices too, and what the clan would make of them.

Reverend Donnelly then said something reporters never expect to hear: He prayed for them. "We pray also for the media, for those who will be reporting upon this event, taking our story to people beyond this community," he said. "Help them to understand our pain. Help them to understand us." With some admirable exceptions—including the *National Post*'s Christie Blatchford, David

Staples of the *Edmonton Journal*, and David Heyman of the *Calgary Herald*—there is little sign that this prayer was answered.

Reverend Donnelly also said, "This event is a life-changing one. It can be an event to make or break this community, this family, or your life. In order to survive, we must support one another. We can do this in many ways. It can be expressed in hugs and smiles, in tears and sadness. . . ." Then he prayed again: "Let peace begin with me . . . to take each moment and live each moment in peace eternally. Let there be peace on earth and let it begin with me."

By the time Karman Willis was killed, Wiebo Ludwig and his follower, Richard Boonstra, had already been facing criminal charges related to the sabotage for six months. Their long road to justice would be littered with roadblocks, some damaging not just to the accused, but also to the RCMP and the oil companies.

Much of the evidence against the clan came from Robert Wraight, a family friend who became an informer. The RCMP turned him, wired him, and set up an explosion, with the tacit cooperation of Alberta Energy, to establish his "credentials" with the clan. During the trial, some of the Wraight tapes were so inaudible that they became a running joke—the Mounties not only couldn't get their man, they couldn't even hear him. Ludwig's sharp lawyers, while poring through the RCMP disclosures, discovered their own useful bomb: an account of how they planned the explosion at an AEC shed. Instantly there were media comparisons with RCMP "dirty tricks" in Quebec in the 1970s. Even sympathetic observers thought it was unwise to set off another explosion in an area where people were already terrified and then pretend it was an eco-terrorist bombing. The Mounties seemed to be adding to community stress rather than relieving it. Gwyn Morgan and the company continued to state that when the RCMP asks for cooperation in catching criminals, the responsible citizen agrees. "I don't care whether it's a drug case or anything else that involves criminal activity, including criminal terrorist activities," says Morgan. "I wouldn't think twice about supporting our military or our police, but I wouldn't design their methods, because that's not our job."[37]

The RCMP tactics were little different, at least in principle, than many other covert operations set up to trap drug dealers and other criminals. They were also legal, but Justice Sterling Sanderman was still critical of the force's lack of judgment. In the end, he dismissed several charges but convicted Ludwig of mischief by destroying property, being in possession of an explosive, counselling to possess an explosive, and attempted possession. Later he sentenced Ludwig to 28 months; Boonstra got only 21 days in jail. There was relief in the Peace, although the haul seemed small for the expenditure of at least $1 million in public money over an investigation that lasted nearly three years.

Morgan says that if he had it to do over again, "I would never meet with him [Ludwig]. I would just stay away from the guy. I didn't realize what kind of person he was. . . . But we got drawn into the situation because we were trying to help, and at the end of the day we became the pawn in the whole process."

Ludwig is an aberration in the Peace country, a zealot who makes up his mind about heroes and villains, and brooks no contradiction. His allegations about the apocalyptic damage done by the industry to his clan remain unproved, and the vast majority of his neighbours share none of his fears. He turned down efforts to study the problem on his farm. Yet in his own terms, Ludwig's strange campaign won some victories, too. He succeeded in spreading a damaging image of oil companies that fit an old and mouldy stereotype. His one useful contribution, perhaps, is that he's made oil executives even more determined to be responsible, to clean up operations wherever they can, and to foster better relations with farmers. Nobody wants to create another Wiebo Ludwig.

A sensible final assessment comes from Dr. Randall Gossen, vice-president of safety, environment, and social responsibility for Nexen Inc. "I can understand the frustrations of landowners, and there are some legitimate concerns. Some farmers and ranchers have got the short end of the stick. But there's never been anything that justifies the actions and approaches that the Wiebo Ludwigs of the world would take."[38]

The Talk

Of all the challenges facing oil and gas companies, few are as important as the need to form cooperative relationships with landowners, environmentalists, Aboriginals, and others affected directly by industry activity. For this the companies need highly skilled and dedicated experts—people like Barry Worbets, for many years the environment manager for Husky Energy and now a private consultant. The challenges of his work are many-sided, and the stakeholders aren't always just members of the community. Sometimes they're company owners who can be full of surprises, as Worbets discovered when he met Li Kai-shing of Hong Kong, 70 per cent owner of Husky and one of the world's richest men.

Worbets knew that Husky was but a small blip in Li Kai-shing's vast network of holdings, so he had no idea what to expect when the owner pulled him aside one day to talk to him about the environment. But he did know that he wouldn't back down—Worbets has an industry-wide reputation for standing his moral ground when his company, or any other, tries to shortchange the environment.

But he quickly found that he had no reason for concern. "Li Kai-shing told me, 'We are not from here. We must do better.' I took him at his word."[1]

That brief conversation cemented Worbets's resolve to make Husky one of the best environmental performers in the petroleum industry. "If an environmentalist hasn't put his job on the line two or three times, he hasn't done his work," he says.

Worbets's career in the petroleum industry began in 1970 when, as a student, he worked on seismic and drilling crews, financing his undergraduate degree as a jug-hound, roustabout, and surveyor.

A determined environmental advocate from the start, Worbets learned to listen first and then quietly present an informed and reasoned response. He contacted those who might be affected by any project, including landowners, environmentalists, and First Nations. For Worbets, the environmental factor was the first consideration at the earliest planning stages of a company development. Respecting public interest was the critical avenue to regulatory approval.

"Barry Worbets is an honourable, honest clear thinker who's a straightforward practitioner of the science," says Dr. Brian Bietz, a former member of the Alberta Energy and Utilities Board and now chairman of the province's Natural Resources Conservation Board. "Anyone who's been in that position, including myself, knows that you make a decision early in your career to determine how best you can effect change."[2] Bietz believes environmentalists have a better opportunity to foster real and lasting change by working within the system. He also insists that it's just as important to have people pressing the buttons outside.

"Both sides face a bit of a trap. On the inside, there's always a risk of getting complacent and saying 'I can live with that,'" says Bietz. "The reverse trap on the outside is that everything becomes a negative, and you have a lot of difficulty recognizing that progress is slow."

The environmentalists on both sides of the industrial fence often work together for common goals, but still end up wary of each other's true motives.

When Barry Worbets first met veteran environmental activist Martha Kostuch, she told him that he was "prostituting" his knowledge for the oil and gas industry. Today, he considers Kostuch a friend and views their jobs as similar.

"My values are the same as hers. I think I would be doing an absolute disservice to owners, executives, and employees if I was to use my ability to do things in a way that wasn't viewed in the broader public interest," insists Worbets. "I've always used my job as the corporate conscience. I've gotten in trouble. I almost had to leave the company because of what I've said."

Ultimately, Worbets started his own environmental consulting business.

"My job was always to get the company to do better and improve its environmental performance. I always said I could effect change more so within the company and I felt very comfortable doing that," says Worbets. "I see the two environmentalists, inside and outside the company, as having the same goals."

Worbets's tenacity and moral conviction ultimately led to his winning one of the most important environmental honours in Canada—Alberta's Emerald Award.

Alberta Wilderness Association director Vivian Pharis was effusive in her praise of Worbets: "Barry has worked tirelessly for environmental stewardship as an integral part of the oil and gas business—he fully deserves the Emerald Award."[3]

Tom Beck was a founding member of the Alberta Wilderness Association and knew Worbets as a student whom he taught at the University of Calgary's Faculty of Environmental Design. Later, Beck recruited Worbets as an environmental affairs employee at Aquitaine Canada (acquired by Canterra Energy, which was later taken over by Husky Energy).

"Since 1980 I have been a close and interested observer of Barry's career and state unequivocally that his interest in and support for sound industrial environmental practices is of the highest order," wrote Beck. "In recent years, his wide practical responsibilities and successes have been matched by his efforts to influence positive changes to environmental policies as they relate to the oil-and-gas industry. A hallmark of Barry's career is his constant effort to ensure that the broad public interest in environment is translated to action at the corporate and field levels."[4]

Pharis describes an incident that showed not only Worbets's dedication to the environment and to organizations like the Alberta Wilderness Association, but also the reality of a company actually sacrificing profits to larger environmental interests. "Back when Tom hired Barry as part of an oil-and-gas company's environmental team," she wrote, "Barry was a fresh young kid, gung-ho and ready to reform the way this industry went about its business. He's never swayed from his early ideals. Barry accepted Tom Beck's early teachings about companies playing a role in communities, about the importance of early public consultation, and about companies being responsible stewards of the land—not just in glossy brochures, but in everyday business.

"The issue was a shut-in, very high sulphur well—running around 60 percent. The well was contentiously located, only a kilometre or so east of the Banff National Park boundary and at the southern end of the AWA's Panther Corners Wildland Recreation Area proposal. Barry knew everything about this well would be contentious. The price of sulphur had risen sharply due to fertilizer sales to South Africa and Canterra wanted to explore the production of this well for sulphur. From an industry standpoint, this whole project was experimental as the sulphur was too thick to flow. From an environmental standpoint, there were extreme wildlife considerations and touchy Aboriginal considerations because of a newly opened road, almost to the park boundary. Barry involved the AWA right away. The AWA encouraged him to hire wildlife and air-emissions specialists to gather information. Barry and Canterra did both.

"On one field trip to the well as it was being tested, Barry and I were astounded and dismayed to encounter a large herd of magnificent Banff Park rams—many were trophy animals and it was already hunting season—licking rig wash off the machinery and piles of drill pipe. We knew that immediate and drastic action was needed. Fortunately (from an environmental viewpoint) it was soon determined that the technology did not exist to economically move this sulphur, so the well was to be shut in again. This left in contention a high-grade road to the well site. The focus of our joint concern soon shifted from the well to the road.

"The AWA asked that in order to protect the bighorns, the road must not only be closed, but also made totally unusable by any sort of vehicle. Barry agreed. Further meetings followed with government agencies and I learned to my astonishment, that an industry road in place is a provincial asset, not to be destroyed. While Fish and Wildlife supported closing the road, Forestry opposed it and was the dominant agency. Tensions rose, with the AWA applying heat. Further meetings that involved industry and the agencies became closed to the public. The AWA leaned heavily on Barry and Canterra, and eventually we won the day. The road was closed and rehabilitated.

"Then the funny thing happened. The AWA had been impressed enough with Barry and Canterra that it nominated Canterra for the Province's Bighorn Award—a rather political award that almost always goes to those in the government trust. Of course a nomination by such a political pariah as the AWA went nowhere. However, word got out to the media that the contentious AWA had nominated an oil-and-gas company for a political award, and that became a big story—one that substantially surpassed the actual awards. In the end, Canterra received far more good political press than did the Bighorn Award winners, all because of who had nominated them.

"Barry and Canterra deserved a provincial award some fifteen to twenty years ago for the piece of work described here. Since the sulphurous Panther Corners well, Barry has continued to work in the same manner, involving the public and making environmental stewardship part of his company's everyday business. Once again, the AWA supports Barry Worbets' nomination for a provincial environmental award, this time, the Emerald Award."

Martha Kostuch recognizes that there are environmentalists like Worbets who work within the petroleum industry, but she still believes that the real environmental job is outside.

"Different approaches from different people at different times work," says Kostuch. "We always weigh and consider what's the best approach."[5] Kostuch and her former husband were Minnesota veterinarians who took advantage of Canadian federal incentives and moved to Rocky Mountain House. Kostuch was beguiled by the beauty of western Alberta and vowed never to leave its mountains, forests, and wildlife. With her four sons (two of them adopted), plus an extra three boys living with her, Kostuch has become a passionate environmentalist because of what she's seen.

"I saw the effects of air pollution on animal health. As emissions went down, I saw its parallel effect on the problems," she says.

Those experiences made Kostuch an activist. She's an earnest, forthright, and opinionated woman who doesn't necessarily trust the industry's attempts to form partnerships with those she believes should remain opponents.

"You have to decide what's the better approach—confrontation or collaboration," she says. "It all depends on the issue and timing and how responsive parties are to issues and concerns and if you have much chance of winning."

One collaborative device that has become very popular and useful is the synergy group—the loose term for informal organizations that form to discuss and debate oil and gas projects. Companies need them to get public input and thus avoid regulatory hearings, while citizens and other stakeholders make their points directly to companies and government officials. They have helped defuse much of the tension surrounding projects and have often led to compromises that everyone can live with.

Yet Kostuch warns that synergy groups can be co-opted and that governments can use them to download their responsibilities.

"Governments can go in and use them to label people who don't want to participate in them as bad," she continues. "Synergy groups are not the way to address all the problems."

Kostuch is worried about the amount of time and energy the groups can sap away in protracted meetings. Yet she does believe that in some cases there are benefits in pulling together all the stakeholders to arrive at some form of consensus.

Kathy Sendall is Petro-Canada's ebullient and energetic senior vice-president for Western Canada. She strongly endorses synergy groups as a mechanism for mutual decision-making and feels they have made great strides over the last few years.

"As a society, I think we're coming to realize that a zero-sum approach to issue resolution, in which there is a clear winner and loser, does not tend to produce the best solutions," says Sendall. "We're realizing that inclusive processes not only avoid alienation and discord—they also tend to produce better, more creative solutions to difficult issues."[6]

The groups have drawbacks, whether they operate as round-table discussions or other consensus-based processes. Certainly, they appear to be more time-consuming than top-down decision-making. Yet this can be misleading too.

"Time spent up front finding a win-win solution often saves time in regulatory or legal procedures down the road," notes Sendall. "In the way of the old adage 'Two heads are better than one,' participation in this process has led to better decision-making and innovative solutions."

Another potential drawback of synergy groups is that sometimes the wrong people end up at the table. This is especially the case when those who claim to represent certain interests or communities actually do not.

"So you need to do your homework and ensure you have solid relationships in place to make synergy groups work," adds Sendall. "I have stressed to our organization over and over again that healthy stakeholder relationships are key to retaining what I call our 'licence to operate.' Healthy stakeholder relationships are not built when there is an issue to resolve and tensions are heightened. They are part of our everyday business and need to be developed and nurtured."

Sendall has made sure that every Petro-Canada operating group in Western Canada has a "stakeholder relationships plan," which is an integral part of the company's business plan.

EnCana CEO Gwyn Morgan believes the growth of synergy groups has been a huge benefit to the industry and society.

"It's not just that you need to be doing the right thing. You have to be seen to be doing the right thing and people have to believe you're doing the right thing," he says.[7]

Even that's not good enough if people don't understand what the oilpatch is up to. Morgan encourages people in the industry to handle issues, concerns, complaints, and inquiries directly, rather than rely on third parties who may not fully fathom the questions, much less the science behind it all.

"The whole issue when you work with communities is that as long as you can deal directly with people, you can usually have success," Morgan adds. "Where it gets to be difficult is when you get third-party outsiders who have their own axe to grind and are actually presenting disinformation."

Bill Clapperton is the vice-president of regulatory, stakeholder, and environmental affairs for Canadian Natural Resources. He finds that multi-stakeholder groups allow information sharing and collaborative learning.

"It brings balance into people and the issues, and it's always to work together," says Clapperton. "Our mission statement at

Canadian Natural is to develop people to work together. It's our biggest strength."[8]

Naturally there are pressures inherent in all such discussions, but Clapperton feels they're overcome through understanding and underscoring common goals.

"There are challenges and we have to keep modifying them," he says. "Everyone cares a lot about the environment and so do we. It's just finding that balance. Do I care about the environment? The answer is yes. But it's not just me, it's our whole company's mission, which is to find ways to minimize our impact on the environment."

When stakeholders cooperate, better industry practices emerge. That same calibre of collaboration is also happening within the petroleum industry as companies work with universities, government, and other research agencies. The goal is innovative, pollution-fighting technology.

"We're really trying to balance everything with new technologies and our ability to modify things," continues Clapperton. "We have to lead the world in some of the technology that we are working on. We can't lose sight of the fact that this is a very important industry that is economically driven and we do live in a global economy. There's no question that there's lots of focus on us, but the fact is that the consumer creates more emissions than the producer."

That reality has only made the job of the Canadian Association of Petroleum Producers more compelling. It is far easier to blame the producer rather than the end-user, especially when the production of petroleum products can create emissions on a far grander scale than a quick ride to the recycling depot in a hot new SUV. Producers have learned through hard experience, public opinion, government regulations, employee concerns, and shareholder questions that communication is crucial and all the stakeholders need to be heard.

"We recognized at CAPP that we had to pay a lot more attention to public opinion. There was a need for constructive engagement with our stakeholders," says vice-president David Pryce.[9] From this emerged the Clean Air Strategic Alliance (CASA). Everyone was committed to make it work, and CASA is now respected as the most successful synergy group of its kind. CASA's focus is air-quality issues, and its lively meetings bring together 23 groups from government, industry, and environmental and health associations, as well as others, to forge cooperative methods to reach mutual goals.

"CASA is a better synergy group than any of the others," says Kostuch. "It truly shares power, and no one participant has more say than any other." Suncor CEO Rick George says simply, "Working together, we have made it work."[10]

CASA's respect within the industry motivated producers to reduce natural gas flaring by 53 per cent, double CASA's flaring reduction goal of 25 per cent for 2001. Within the next few years flaring is expected to drop by 70 per cent, and CASA's current challenge of reducing natural gas venting will have to meet the same stringent goals.

"CASA is very effective working with industry, the public, and NGOs [non-government organizations] in exchanging information so there's stronger understanding of concerns and opportunities and ways of integrating them into more effective outcomes," explains Nexen CEO Charlie Fischer.[11]

One influential NGO participating in CASA is the Pembina Institute for Appropriate Development. Pembina's director of Energy Watch, Tom Marr-Laing, sits on the CASA board.

"It becomes an issue of how enlightened and informed management are and how well they filter that down the line," says Marr-Laing. "It all starts at the top and is tempered by how much priority the CEO places on the environment and by how much money the senior officers are willing to target as they tackle environmental issues."

"The mutual challenge is how far can we move the company, and that varies," adds Marr-Laing. "Let's see where we can get to, and then see what we need to do to get there. It all depends on how fertile the ground is to work in."[12]

Marr-Laing is thankful for industry leaders who make environmental issues a corporate responsibility and lead their wary or less enlightened colleagues to the path of environmental respect and corporate social responsibility. And while Marr-Laing has reservations about the industry, he feels it has improved since the early 1990s.

Certainly CAPP has been instrumental in that shift, backed by heavyweight members such as EnCana, Nexen, Petro-Canada, Shell Canada, Chevron, Canadian Natural, Conoco, Suncor, and Syncrude. In 1999, CAPP started its stewardship program, which urges its 150 member companies to "continually improve their environment, health and safety performance and to report their progress to stakeholders." After an introductory period during which compliance was voluntary, by January 2003 all companies must meet these five strategic goals:

1. Improve operations in environmentally, economically, and socially responsible ways.
2. Communicate and consult with stakeholders about company plans and activities.
3. Comply with recommended operating practices.
4. Report company performance against benchmarking measures.
5. Verify the effectiveness of company environment, health and safety management systems, and performance.[13]

Brian Bietz, who has long believed the program should be mandatory, says it will now be even more effective. "We'll see a rapid increase in performance," he feels. "What gets measured gets fixed. It's that simple."

About four years ago, CAPP organized an industry–landowner task force to determine current problems and develop feasible solutions. They quickly identified the problems: the consultation process; inconsistent information; behavioural and environmental concerns; and technical challenges such as groundwater supply and quality.

"We identified a whole range of issues and said, 'What can we do about that? What are the five or six things we can do over the year?'" says David Pryce. CAPP set out to improve communications and organized a synergy group conference so that regional and community organizations could tackle issues directly with producers in their areas. CAPP also worked with the Alberta Energy and Utilities Board and other groups to develop the Appropriate Dispute Resolution process, which brings together industry and landowners to try to understand each other's objections and generate workable solutions.

Bietz acknowledges that some producers have established strong relationships with landowners. But Bietz also believes that many producers deny the fundamental reality that the well is being drilled in someone's backyard. He wants producers to understand that rural Albertans put up with "a lot of stuff. If you asked anyone in the industry if they had to put up with the same disservice in their own homes, they would find it unacceptable."[14]

Bietz cites exasperating practices like using a landowner's water lines, or ignoring a squeaky pump-jack just outside an owner's bedroom window, or knocking on the farm door at three in the morning because someone's driven into the ditch—again. Bietz believes that because the company is paying the owner to operate on the land, it develops a proprietary attitude that offends farmers.

"That's not the way the rural area works," advises Bietz. "It's about relationships, and if you create the right one, then money is irrelevant. Oil and gas men have difficulty shifting over into someone else's perspective."

Respect is the beginning of a better relationship with landowners; to get it, companies need to remember always that they're drilling and exploring at someone else's home.

Murray Edwards is one of the country's most influential oilmen and he strongly supports CAPP's stewardship program. He sees it as a clear example of the industry working to improve relations with landowners and communities. The program also provides innovative solutions for companies trying to manage environmental challenges.

"I think that if you meet with the stakeholders, especially the landowners, you'll see that oil companies on the whole try to be very positive in dealing with problems," says Edwards. "I think there is a lot more dialogue today and most companies are very proactive in trying to find beneficial and cost-effective ways to deal with the challenges. In rural Alberta the industry is thought of very highly."[15]

Edwards is right. As noted earlier, 80 per cent of Albertans polled feel the oil and gas industry's environmental performance has improved.[16] This bodes well for producers because the total number includes all of Alberta—both urban and rural areas. In past studies, rural residents gave the industry higher grades than city-dwellers did. In part that's because farmers and ranchers often relied on the industry to get them through a paltry crop or a desultory winter. The old adage—oil was the best crop the farmer ever had—was too often true.[17]

"There's an appreciation in Western Canada for what the oil and gas industry does in giving back to the community and the economy and being environmentally sensitive," explains Edwards. "Can they do a better job? Absolutely. The proof is in the action. We strive for excellence."

CAPP's former manager of environmental affairs, Gary Webster, points out that people who work in the oil companies are citizens first. They live in the same area where the facilities are located and are hardly likely to put their environment in peril. They also have families and friends who live in those communities, and all have been instrumental in pressing for respect, communication, and honesty in relations between industry and neighbours.

"The city folk never had much to do with the industry. Typically it was farmers, ranchers, and trappers. Now we have seen quite an exodus from the city of people building second homes close to oil production," says Webster.[18]

Edwards also points out that most people in the cities seldom come into contact with oil and gas production unless they visit or move to the country. They don't have the experience or the history—which in the main has been positive—that rural areas have with producers.

Dr. Roger Gibbins is a noted Canadian authority on Western Canada and heads up the Canada West Foundation, an academic think tank. He agrees that as urbanites move to the country in search of a rural paradise, the potential for conflict escalates. Yet he applauds the industry for its changes.

"It does seem that the industry has been pretty successful in trying to move the polarity between environmental protection and the oilpatch. That was just such a part of our conventional wisdom that these were on two different sides," says Gibbins. "The Canadian oil industry is doing what appears to be a pretty effective job."[19]

Bietz still believes that the industry hasn't fully come to grips with a different public that wants more hard facts on oil and gas developments and their broad impact. With global communication and the Internet, the public is far more sophisticated than in the past and has access to all kinds of information.

"The guys I talk with deal in derivatives and futures markets and then arrange multimillion-dollar loans with their bankers for new developments. And these are the farmers," says Bietz. "The oil and gas companies have to get around this fact. Plus, lots of the farmers they're talking to work in the patch part-time. They have to have data—no more can it be 'Trust me, it's safe.' If they can work those things through the synergy groups, then it will do them a ton of good."[20]

That's already happening with many oilpatch leaders. Nexen's Charlie Fischer doesn't like anything sprung on people who live where his company operates. He wants information fully available to the communities and synergy groups so the projected development and its ramifications are readily understood.

"Wherever we're conducting major activities, we meet with local communities, tell them what we're doing, schedule open houses, and ask questions. We conduct a very integrated and open process," he says. "Now the community is your partner, and there shouldn't be surprises if you're conducting your business properly. It's an evolution of understanding and treating people the way you want to be treated yourself if you were living there."[21]

When most Canadian companies go global, they try to take their sense of corporate responsibility abroad, including their vision, philosophy, and best practices. The last thing they want is to be caught up in a war or accused of propping up a savage regime. Their reputation and stock value slither. Talisman Energy's stake in Sudan produced plenty of oil along with accusations of abetting a vicious government. Even after Talisman put the property on the block, its stock continued to slip.

"The whole issue around globalization for me is an interest," says Charlie Fischer, whose company, Nexen, has operations in Yemen. "When we meet with government officials in Yemen, they hold our company up as [an example of] how to do business globally. When I met with the union representative in Yemen, he just wanted to say thank you for the jobs, and how they were treated.

"But that's not news. What gets reported in the media is corruption and collusions. Companies like ours work really hard to be effective in countries where we operate around the world. We build relationships and enhance the quality of life in those communities."

Producers also believe they can enhance the quality of life within Aboriginal communities in Canada upon whose lands they increasingly hope to explore and drill. Companies are signing memoranda of understanding (MOUs) that respect the Aboriginal cultures and offer viable business partnerships. The MOUs stress economic development as well as employment and entrepreneurial opportunities. They promise to invest in community health, education, and social programs. And they recognize the role of the elders in decision-making. The MOUs' importance is usually reflected in a historic pipe ceremony that is led by the community elders. Crucial to all MOUs is respect for the environment and a recognition of the land as sacred to the cultural heritage of Aboriginal people.

Lawyer Jerome Slavik applauds producers who take the time to build communications and relationships with Aboriginal communities, pointing out that if they don't, the lawyers will take over and fill that gap. Producers know that they have to convey the environmental, social, and economic impacts of any development while also appreciating the intricate political dynamics surrounding a project's approval.

"The whole process of accessing, managing, and monitoring has taken such huge leaps in the past 10 years with the improvement in the sophistication and understanding of the environmental impact of development," observes Slavik. "The Pembina Institute began as a critic of the petroleum industry. Now they are criticized as being co-opted because they work with all the stakeholders involved in a development. In the 1980s, the whole idea of 'stakeholder' was new."[22]

Slavik recalls the classic moment when Suncor referred to Fort McKay First Nation as a neighbour sharing a common airshed.

"For a company to say 'We breathe the same air'—this occurred in the mid-'80s—was ground-breaking. Prior to that, the air was seen as one big disposal pit," says Slavik. "When it became apparent that the Aboriginal communities could use the situation to tie up the industry and the regulators, it became in the interest of the regulators to actively mediate. The regulators would make the dialogue happen, or go directly to facilitate it, or stop the process until it happened."

For First Nations, this meant leverage. Community consultation with Aboriginal peoples became crucial. The regulators focused on fair discussion and due process, and rarely had to go to a lengthy judicial hearing. Their goal was to accommodate the interests and concerns of all participants through non-adversarial discussions. Regulators called upon expert evidence and helped producers develop best practices, incorporating the most current and yet cost-effective technologies available. The discussion encouraged in-depth debate over environmental consequences coupled with effective management. In the end, Aboriginal communities learned how to take advantage of that process to further their goals.

Slavik also points out that the B.C. government could learn from companies like EnCana, Suncor, and Syncrude and their progressive relationships with Aboriginal communities.

"The reality is that companies need to develop relationships with the Aboriginal communities," explains Slavik. "Otherwise there's a bitterness and suspicion and a sense of exclusion that outside lawyers can capitalize upon to build even further wedges between all the parties."

The best producers hire people who forge strong relationships with Aboriginal communities to enhance the level of trust and understanding. The ultimate goal is to bring Aboriginal peoples into the industry through viable employment and business opportunities.

"Unless First Nations people see they're getting some of their interests met—environmental, economic, and social—they will only focus on blocking the development," adds Slavik.

Chief Jim Boucher, long-time leader of the Fort McKay First Nation, is pleased with the partnerships between industry and First Nations, and his community is directly engaged in learning administrative and technological skills provided by industry experts.

"The goal is economic development for the betterment of community," says Boucher. "We're developing our business front, and a variety of our members are actively engaged in business relationships with industry."[23]

That's for sure. Fort McKay First Nation has a transportation company, an environmental service, and a general contracting business focusing on heavy equipment. There's a geotechnical company; Fort McKay industrial park; Fort McKay Trucking, which handles huge tanker trucks; and First North Catering, which can manage a camp of 5,000 people.

Boucher believes there's been a massive shift within the oilpatch, where the social and environmental consequences have now become an integral part of the industry's economic equation. By becoming proactive, the Fort McKay First Nation was able to take back its community and protect its future. By listening to an important stakeholder and holding synergy discussions, the industry rebuilt its image, restored a crucial relationship with its Aboriginal neighbours, and developed one of the most important energy sources on the planet. For both parties, an era of mutual respect and understanding had begun.

"When we actively made plans to resolve issues after communications broke down, we went to the regulatory forum," explains Boucher. "After doing that numerous times, it was recognized by industry and the community that going through the regulatory process was not the best way to resolve concerns. From the company point of view, the negative public relations and the costs of regulatory review were quite onerous.

"From our perspective, we never won, even if we won the battle, because the ultimate outcome was not in our favour. It was a lose-lose situation for both parties. As a result, we've engaged in a new type of process, complete with an attitude of mutual respect and win-win."

Boucher likes the new approach in which issues are identified and resolved before the proposal moves forward. The community sets its own priorities so that it too benefits from the project. This dramatic change has made Boucher a booster of producers who respect Aboriginal cultures and development.

"Industry is taking a leadership approach to dealing with Aboriginal communities," he states. "They've gone far beyond what was done before in the '60s, '70s, and '80s, when they would decide and then defend their project. Now they're doing their business with consultations and then mutual decisions. Consultation is very important in terms of how their project will proceed.

"This is a major shift. Before, they just went ahead. Now, they want to work with communities in a positive way. There's no doubt industry has taken a lead in establishing positive relations with us."

In fact, Boucher challenges governments and other industries and businesses to follow the petroleum industry's lead. He'd like to see the government make an investment in community housing and infrastructure to mitigate the social impact of population influx following developments.

Boucher would especially like the federal government to resolve outstanding land claims: "It would give us the foundation to enter into the next economic stream, where our land and natural resources would provide us with another form of economic wherewithal for our people."

He applauds the petroleum industry for investing far beyond the economic arena in Aboriginal people and communities. Producers have provided a social network of support systems in addition to a day care, school, and educational and elders' programs.

"The industry's leadership is exemplary in comparison with what goes on across the country," states Boucher. "This industry leads in environmental issues and new technologies. It has developed technologies to ensure environmental concerns are being met.

"It leads in terms of developing relationships within the Aboriginal communities, compared with companies across the country. We've managed to obtain significant benefits once we've become engaged. Aboriginal peoples participate in the mainstream of the industry. That's not the way it is in business across the country, and we see very little of this. The petroleum industry is doing a lot in terms of supporting Aboriginal communities."

Boucher cited some impressive figures. On the economic front, $212 million will go to Aboriginal businesses in 2002, up dramatically from $60 million in 1998. The industry will employ 1,200 Aboriginal people, up from 800 in 1998. After spending six years in the industry, an Aboriginal worker earns an average income of $64,000.

While many Native leaders have forged a successful economic, social, and environmental relationship with the industry through the MOUs they've signed, environmentalists are still displeased with the whole idea of oilsands development.

Martha Kostuch has only cautious praise for producers and their dramatic reductions in gas flaring. She is especially critical of oilsands projects.

"I'd like to see that development curtailed and cease any expansion. They should look at reducing what is already on the table. There is no way to make it sustainable," maintains Kostuch.[24] She labels "piddly" the positive environmental changes the industry has achieved through technological innovation and public will.

"These are small baby steps, and they haven't really tackled big problems with land use. It's not good enough. We need to look at getting off the fix on fossil fuels. We're addicted to fossil fuels."

Kostuch wants to change all that and brings that conviction to the many industry synergy meetings she attends. Her message is very clear.

"We have to explore and develop the alternatives. We need to put more effort into demand-side management and reducing our consumption. In 50 years there should be no consumption of fossil fuels for energy in the world. The bottom line is that we've made some improvements, but we still have a long way to go."[25]

Syncrude CEO Eric Newell disagrees sharply with Kostuch and other environmental activists who want to curtail all development. He sees the oilsands projects as a path to economic renewal for Aboriginals in the area as well as contributing to the Canadian economy as a whole.

"These environmentalists just plain want to shut us down. They don't even want a debate about how to do things better, unlike the environmentalists at Pembina [Institute]," says Newell. "We need to identify all the efforts we are making, such as reducing our energy use, to be environmentally helpful. The environmentalists would still rather have us, though, than nuclear power."[26]

Kostuch does acknowledge that "there are areas where CAPP is doing a lot of good things."[27] That in itself is music to the ears of Greta Raymond, Petro-Canada's dynamic vice-president of human resources, environment, health, and safety.

Raymond does her part by working with environmentalists at the Pembina Institute who introduced Petro-Canada to the concept of "Life Cycle Value Assessment." This model for eco-efficiency focuses on more value to society for less use of limited resources and less damage to the environment.

"The LCVA is a business analysis and decision-making tool that combines environmental information for the full life cycle of a product or system, with financial cost-benefit information, to enable better decision-making," explains Raymond. "We agreed to try it because we were doing some work with the Pembina Institute around oilsands. The Life Cycle Value Assessment has opened people's eyes."[28]

Raymond finds that the model can strengthen the financial and business reasons behind decisions. It gives a "cradle-to-grave" understanding of environment, health, and safety impacts as well as risks, and can also improve the technical designs for a project.

Syncrude's Eric Newell is a leader whose business acumen is sought across the country. Over the years he's built a solid reputation with stakeholders, and especially with the Aboriginal communities. Part of the mutual respect comes from his own ethnicity, he feels. "I'm Irish. It's three steps forward, two steps back," he grins.[29]

While Newell is pleased with the strength of his relationships with Aboriginal peoples and Syncrude's record of Aboriginal employment, he readily admits to some setbacks.

"The areas where we haven't been as successful are in the professions and management," Newell says. "Twenty years from now, if Aboriginal peoples aren't represented in management in Syncrude, we won't have been successful."

At Syncrude, Newell wants Aboriginals to reach their full potential. He sees this as critical to those communities reaping their full share from resource development. All Syncrude managers take cross-cultural training to help them understand and appreciate Aboriginal culture. Newell worked with local chiefs and heads of Metis groups to hand-pick their best people, including students, to become role models for their communities. Education is a priority for Newell, and he met many times with Keyano College in Fort McMurray to develop scholarships and other funding for Aboriginal training.

"Everyone had a responsibility. The Aboriginal responsibility was to provide the talent pool. There's a lot of strong entrepreneurial skills within Native peoples," Newell points out. "Each of the leaders articulated their vision for their communities. Elders are wonderful people and genuinely concerned about the environment and the land. They asked me how I can be so sure that I can deal with all the issues. I said that even if we were wrong, at Syncrude we would make it right."[30]

The leaders got together often, discussed the issues, and selected members of the Aboriginal community who would work in Syncrude's environmental group. Newell believes the best defence against any who raise the environmental flag is to devote money, skill, and resources to leaving as light a footprint on the land as possible.

"At Syncrude, we have trees and boreal forest growing on a tailings pond. There's grassland pasture with a roaming herd of 300 bison. We have a log cabin on that land and bring people there to see what we're doing in reclamation. Elders, when they see it, become very comfortable knowing we know what we're doing. We put the land back into excellent condition."

Syncrude created an industry group with the community and the Athabasca Tribal Council that works on benefit sharing, employment, education, and business development. Syncrude also provides funds for Aboriginal groups to research issues of concern.

"We don't believe this is just something you do for regulatory approval, but it's part of an ongoing relationship," says Newell. "The money is very well spent by the industry. We can't do just an average or good job—we have to do an outstanding job with our stakeholders. We're working together with environmentalists and Aboriginals."

Certainly the Alberta Energy and Utilities Board requires producers to consult with local communities before a project moves forward. But there are other reasons too—producers want allies, not foes.

"The reality is that you need the support of the community. That's why we work hard in areas of Aboriginal employment and education," Newell says. "We've made the commitment that local people share equally in the benefits of oilsands development. How could we even say that if they weren't representative in our work force?"

Syncrude's workforce is 13 per cent Aboriginal, and even when the company was cutting back, it continued to hire and keep Aboriginal employees.

"Today, we're probably the star in Canada and have the best relationship between industry and Aboriginal groups. We have 700 on our site, and all are highly skilled, highly paid, and excellent employees," explains Newell. "Syncrude also benefits because they aren't going to leave here. This is their ancestral home. We help Aboriginal entrepreneurs to become self-sustaining. We work in a very meaningful way on the environmental standards and on the benefits side. We don't sacrifice our standards and we're not perfect, but in the long run, we all benefit."

Newell and his family became active members of the community. Like Chief Boucher, Newell wants government to play a stronger role by investing in infrastructure and housing. He worries about the slippery slope of inadequate housing and consequent social ills.

"For industry, we need the right to operate, and we need the support of the public," he says. "But if we deal with Aboriginal communities the right way, they become a great source of employment and business opportunities. Aboriginals get good jobs and careers, develop stronger communities, and are more able to sustain themselves. If we can ultimately all be successful, then there really aren't any drawbacks."

Newell's deepest respect goes to the elders, who are the real power and source of inspiration for Aboriginal communities. Native cultures revere their elders for their deep wisdom and insight. It's the elders who take the long-term approach in any industry proposal and who examine whether it means their people will wholeheartedly be included or simply be used for political gain and then discarded.

Rick George, CEO of another prominent and historic player in the oilsands, attributes the relationships and discussions his company held with Aboriginal peoples as setting the stage for Suncor's overall strategy toward community involvement.

"I take no personal credit for this, but I think our experience at Suncor was led by the folks in the oilsands," George explains. "When we did our first expansion, we said: 'Listen, this issue of putting on the table what you're going to do, and then defending it, probably is not a really great approach.'

"Think about something that happens in your neighbourhood where the developer wants to do x, y, or z. You feel a lot better if the guy comes and talks to you. Or if your neighbour is going to do a big modification, it's just nicer if you go across the street and say, 'I know this is going to cause some problems, but I'm going to modify my house, and there'll be a little confusion around for a couple of months. This is what it's going to look like.'

"And if you think about how you approach your own neighbourhood, the same thing applies, and that's what worked for us at Fort McMurray. Go on up to the stakeholder and say, 'This is kind of what we have in mind to do, and we're here to get your input.'

"Then you're not on the defensive and now you're trying to understand what people's concerns are and how you might mitigate those. You're never going to make 100 per cent of the people you deal with happy. But the fact that you're open and willing to talk and listen and make change when it makes sense has been for us a real positive experience."[31]

George feels that community consultation and suggestions from synergy groups have produced a regulatory process that is far more collaborative for Suncor and much less confrontational.

"I actually think it has helped us come to better decisions. It has really helped the community in terms of 'It's not an us or them' kind of thing. Lots of benefits spin off," he says.

George is a big fan of synergy groups even though he's often at the centre of some heated discussions. The bottom line is that anyone with an interest in a project gets to air his or her concerns and suggest workable solutions. In particular, the Pembina Institute has helped Suncor, among many other petroleum companies, develop socio-ecological models that provide frameworks for understanding the long-term implications of a project.

"Our relationship with the Pembina Institute, where they push us around and we don't agree on everything, is actually healthy," explains George. "I've always found this to be positive. Not that you agree, but the dialogue is very important. We still get people who really want to get into the litany 'The sky is falling, the water is dirty.' Then that gets into a polarized debate. And that is not where Suncor is, and not where the world is. What we all know is that we can improve and our job is to do that."

George opts for the high road and heads away from the highly political banter, focusing instead on making the project and the process better.

"I do think that the world is not going to hell in a handbasket. It is not. Now, is there plenty of room for improvement? Absolutely, absolutely. And that's where we ought to be working."

There can be drawbacks to any in-depth discussions involving the airing of issues among so many stakeholders. At the beginning, some producers even feel powerless because they're not controlling the agenda. They also have a healthy concern that their competitors are listening for corporate secrets. Still, confidential company projects are first aired in the privacy of their own boardrooms where, presumably, they will also develop the strategy for the very public meetings.

"This is a competitive business, and your competitors can see what you're doing because you're now public," George says. "They can see your move and then can plot their own. That's something I'm a little touchy about. I think when you're more open you're a little bit more vulnerable to attack. This is not an oilpatch issue—it's a human issue in terms of any time you hold yourself open you always feel slightly vulnerable, don't you? Legally, the industry has a right to drill on the farmer's land. But you have a responsibility to treat the landowner the way you want to be treated."

The relationship between environmentalists and producers is much like that between Fred Astaire and Ginger Rogers. He brought respect and she brought the sex appeal. When they worked together, it was magic. What environmental groups bring to the dance floor is credibility. Corporations provide the talent and money. The fact that they can cooperate shows a capacity for learning and understanding that has swept through some—not yet all—of the tony petroleum towers.

Environmentalists see that companies can make good things happen, if there's a corporate will. Producers gain credibility by implementing mutual goals. That's synergy, and it exudes a kind of community magic when it works.

"Companies are made up of people, and our employees care about the same things that environmentalists do," says Gordon Lambert, Suncor vice-president of sustainable development. "On that more human level, when the environmental community gets to know the people who actually work for these firms, putting a face to these companies often breaks down the barriers.

"In a society we'll always have a segment of the public that has an anti-industrial development attitude. In a democracy we'll always have a full spectrum of views on economic development, environmental protection, and social issues. We respect that and do not dismiss it. If individuals express that view and do it within the law, it's their right."[32]

Lambert, like many colleagues throughout the industry, states with passion that he is an environmentalist. He considers his life's work the search for solutions that reconcile a strong economy with a healthy environment.

"I can't see an industrial sector in Canada any more engaged in environmental issues than the oil and gas industry," he says. "We do interact with communities across the country, and no one takes these concerns lightly at all. I take a lot of pride working in this business."

The best companies want to be the developer of choice. The competition is fierce, and producers with a strong corporate conscience and a will to do the right thing with communities and other environmental partners have a built-in edge.

Brian MacNeill, the former CEO of Enbridge, recalls working with numerous groups, especially since the pipeline business interacts with tens of thousands of people and their properties. He found it all to be an enormous advantage for the company.

"One of our right-of-way people shows up and discusses issues—we constantly do that—and there's a benefit there for us. They're our eyes and ears, these landowners," maintains MacNeill.[33]

In fact, he can't think of any drawback to community consultations and synergy discussions. Certainly the whole process takes some time initially, which might delay the project "a little" and increase some costs. For MacNeill those were all minor annoyances compared to the advantages of listening to people and coming up with workable solutions.

"We've had to deal with some hostile people," says MacNeill. "If we have a pipeline break, we don't always follow the niceties of knocking on the door. We start talks with a local person and in most cases you can reason with people. We have a trapper on staff in the Norman Wells area of the Northwest Territories who talks to other trappers to see if we're messing up the traplines."

Over the span of his career in the industry, MacNeill has seen an easing of relations between the petroleum industry and environmentalists as people become more informed and conscious of social issues.

"We'll always have the extremists, but I'm an optimist, and I see people who are coming up in the industry having a broader approach than some of the old guard that built the industry," he says.

Ray Woods is the senior operating officer of resources for Shell Canada and the past chairman of CAPP. He's a big supporter of synergy groups and believes they're the integral ingredient to a viable business recipe.

"They're an enormously positive development," he says. "We support and are active in them because they offer hope. They allow you to better understand the stakeholders around your operations and allow them to understand you. If things go wrong, you have a level of trust that gives everyone time to react rather than point fingers."[34]

Woods also recognizes the tremendous time, energy, and resources that are required, especially from volunteers. Synergy groups would evaporate into a cloud of anger if there was nothing to show for their dedicated commitment. That's why the onus is on industry to prove that all the public's time and work, usually unpaid, yield a worthy project and a healthy environment.

All these company leaders readily acknowledge that the business leaves a giant footprint that must be erased through innovative reclamation efforts. They are intimately aware of the consequences—environmental, social, and economic—that their developments deliver. And they react sharply when anyone suggests they might betray this public trust.

The industry is the lightning rod for debate on environmental responsibility, and the oilpatch is riddled with sour relationships built on anger and mistrust. But the industry has also triggered a massive change within its own perimeters, knowing that it is judged not by the best, but by the worst performer. Industry leaders now stress communication and cooperation as they rebuild their reputation to reflect what employees, associates, and many communities believe it to be: a responsible corporate citizen.

"I'm not sure you can say someone is an environmentalist and someone else is not," says Michael Tims, the respected CEO of investment bankers Peters & Co. "In general, oil and gas companies want to be on the good side, for a market benefit, a public relations benefit, and an employee benefit. By making environmental responsibility an explicit part of what you as a company do, people feel very reassured."[35]

When oil and gas companies build this kind of thinking into their strategic goals, they prod and even embarrass others to do the same. They use best practices that include the latest technological innovations, because the oilpatch leaders are determined to change the way the industry is perceived.

"Companies have gotten much more sophisticated in addressing community relations and environmental issues in a constructive way. Everybody learns," adds Tims. "But if somebody comes to a discussion with a fixed view against the industry, it's hard to collaborate on any development that will make them happy, especially if there is a philosophical or political mindset that is very different.

"So you ask what the concerns are and how to deal with them in a reasonable manner. You get to the specific process that they're concerned about and deal with the factors that they object to, so that the standard of a reasonable person would be met."

Dean Lien has farmed in southern Alberta, near Lethbridge, for 35 years and has for the last four years acted as the Alberta government-appointed farmers' advocate. He deals directly with industry–farmer problems, as well as oil spills and reclamation needs.

"The oil industry is concerned about its image and is doing things better than it was for a long time, in terms of cleaning up and in the way they treat farmers," says Lien. "What we try to do is empower the people on the land and teach them how to go through certain steps. Farmers are getting more knowledgeable and request more information."[36]

"When you go back to some of the well sites of the 1950s, it was pretty disastrous. In general the companies are better. There's still the attitude of some of the land people [from the oil companies] that they think the land is theirs, and the farmers are tough to deal with. When somebody comes onto their land, farmers expect some respect, and I think they're getting more of that."

As the farmers' advocate, Lien meets with the farmers and industry to try to resolve problems before any development proceeds. When the company and a landowner meet and have a dispute, they can use the EUB's Alternative Dispute Resolution (ADR) process to do their best to arrive at a consensus. Since its inception in January 2001, the ADR has succeeded in settling 70 per cent of the contentious issues.

"For us, ADR was a non-confrontational way to deal with issues that were becoming roadblocks," Jeri Kerluke, a farmer, told the Canadian Association of Petroleum Producers. "I was able to speak frankly and make my concerns known. As a result, I got things done that I needed to have done. The ADR process is really one of the best ways individuals can make an impact."[37]

Jeri Kerluke farms in Millarville, near Calgary. Kerluke had worried about emissions and water quality, especially since her family grows everything they eat. As soon as she heard that more sour gas wells were going to be drilled near her farm, she objected. Kerluke and the company went to ADR. The process opened up communication between the two and gave Kerluke a comfort zone when the company established air- and wind-monitoring systems on her property.

Dean Lien notes that "all these farmers worry about air and water. There's a big concern that the oil industry is using water for flooding and injecting steam [into heavy-oil recovery techniques]. I think the industry has to prove that they don't use the aquifers the farmers need. It all gets down to a situation of 'not in my back-yard,' which happens all the time. But I think that, environmentally, the industry is being more responsible. About 90 per cent of the farmers are able to work with industry."

Today, more technological breakthroughs have helped the farmer–industry relationship, especially heli-portable seismic and GPS (global positioning system), and directional drilling, which is crucial in irrigated areas. (These innovations are further discussed in Chapter 6.)

"Anyone with a concern can call us," adds Lien, who also administers the Water Well Restoration or Replacement Program, which oversees industry effects on water wells. The farmers, community members, and an Alberta government environment representative meet to examine whether any damage to a farmer's well has been caused by industry seismic or drilling actions. In 2000, the program reimbursed 22 of the 26 who applied for compensation.

One of the most successful stakeholder associations is the Sundre Petroleum Operators Group. Considered the flagship for more than 50 synergy groups, SPOG became the model for serious discussions and workable solutions.

"Synergy groups bring people together to learn about and understand each other," farmer and SPOG member David Brown told CAPP. "If there's a concern, it belongs to all stakeholders. Getting around the table is important because it gives us the opportunity to look at options and seek solutions for everyone involved."[38]

Frank Dabbs is an author, consultant, and business columnist who lives near Sundre, northwest of Calgary. He remembers SPOG's origins about 12 years ago, as a mutual aid society with little community participation. The Caroline-Sundre district was one of the province's most intensively developed petroleum areas. At the same time, land use diversified rapidly. Cattle operations increased, logging escalated, and environmental tourism took off with activities like fishing, camping, hiking, and horseback riding. All the while, the population rose as city-dwellers searched for their country paradise.

"So conflicts developed, and all these things that oil companies did that weren't being noticed now were noticed," says Dabbs. "Initially it was a mutual aid thing with companies like Nova and Shell who said, 'Let's have a 1-800 line' for oil spills and such."[39]

Two things happened. Shell decided to expand its Caroline gas-processing plant, and those who were opposed to its initial construction got angry all over again. Then a Nova pipeline blew up, just a short walk from the Shell Caroline plant, when two high-pressure lines that crossed suddenly ruptured. The damage was contained, but it was a wake-up siren for the community.

"SPOG created a community affairs working group and set a 600-square-mile boundary. They appointed representatives from all the rural community associations in that area and opened the door to citizens and companies who wanted in," says Dabbs.

The SPOG vision was a long-term relationship based on mutual trust, honesty, and respect. They shared information and expected that all stakeholders, including industry, would benefit from the outcome. The group developed a process, complete with performance measures, that they wanted met.

"And if you can't meet them, they want to know why," says Dabbs. "The companies that got it kept out of regulatory hearings and saw community problems resolved. This little model of companies and communities at the table created synergy."

Companies became bold in their community relations and made promises that weren't even part of the regulatory process. SPOG raised the bar on mutual communication and trust. In turn, people within the communities increased their knowledge about the industry, its changing technology, and its transforming attitude.

"A scientist from Prudential Steel explained how they made steel that was resistant to sour gas. Another guy described how gas-gathering systems are laid and how the route is picked," says Dabbs. "We had an unwritten contract that the community would set the standards and the company would meet them and, if they couldn't, would have to explain why."

Even though Dabbs had 30 years of experience working within and writing about the industry, he found there was much to learn about the technology and the economics of being environmentally responsible.

"Now they're showing the community that they're prepared to be on the leading edge—to spend money and take the technological risk," adds Dabbs.

SPOG has moved far beyond its original goal and now encourages meetings with all who are involved in emergency response plans. SPOG's annual Neighbours' Day has become a marquee event, attracting over 800 attendees to lunch and discuss environmental issues and emergency action.

"SPOG led the way," says Lien. "Of course, we'll never get all people to agree. There are situations where some farmers were treated wrongly and they'll never get over it. But some good things are coming about. I think we're being more appreciated by industry."

Another big fan of groups like SPOG is Gary Sargent, the general manager of the Alberta Cattle Commission. Sargent readily acknowledges that there will always be challenges between industry and landowners because they're both competing for the same piece of turf. The industry needs access to the surface to get below, while the farmer or rancher needs that very surface to grow crops or graze livestock. Both need water, with farmers using 70 per cent of surface water in Alberta for irrigation. The oil and gas industry holds between 2 and $2\frac{1}{2}$ per cent of the issued water licences but uses only 40 to 60 per cent of that share. An independent study done for CAPP points out that a considerable effort is being made by producers to use salty water from deep wells, which is of no use to farmers. But the perception is that the producers are blithely taking scarce water from farmers and ranchers whose parched land and thirsty stock need it more.[40]

"The regulators need to do what they can to ensure the industry minimizes its impacts on landowners. The oil industry has to deal fairly, openly, and honestly with landowners over the operations they are planning and what the impacts may be," says Sargent. "It always sets up the potential for conflict. The goal is to have oil and gas operations that don't interfere with the landowner's business."[41]

Sargent likes the improvements he's seen over the last few years but worries that some of the oil companies might not be able to fulfil what has now become expected practice in environmental management and landowner disclosure.

"We've done a number of things that mitigate conflict, but some of the challenges continue to be that Western Canadian exploration tends to have fallen to smaller companies that don't necessarily have the same professional capabilities on board to do all the things that a major company is able to do.

"But I've certainly seen good cooperation. Maybe we just got to know each other better at different levels than what had been the case previously. The cattle and oil industries work better together today than ever before."

Sargent cites improved regulations and protocol with regard to sour gas processing facilities, technological advances and enhanced standards, and gas flaring reductions. He's especially enthusiastic about the Animal Health Investigator, a program that hires an independent veterinarian to examine animal health problems that could be related to the oil and gas industry. The investigator is funded by petroleum, agriculture, and government groups and is confidential, cost-free, and open to all livestock owners.

As editor of *Oilweek* magazine, Gordon Jaremko is considered the dean of energy writers, a journalist who has earned the respect of everyone connected with the oilpatch. He sees a positive change in the relationship between the industry, the community, and the environment. As an example, he cites Barry Worbets's work while at Husky, overseeing the environmentally sensitive Moose Mountain project in the Kananaskis country (along the southwest Alberta border). Plans were developed for a wildlife habitat, pinpointing the protection of grizzlies.

Worbets's motto—be a good neighbour—meant starting consultation early and often with landowners, First Nations, recreational users, and NGOs. There were aesthetic, visual, and noise considerations. Any development had to minimize its footprint, its impact, and any disturbance. That required innovation and a current understanding of the most advanced technology available.

"How thoroughly is this change pervading the industry?" asks Jaremko. "You'll always get the companies that are very sophisticated in this, like Shell or Chevron or EnCana. The issue is: Is that spreading throughout the industry? Now companies have to do diplomatic work at quite a wide radius to get projects through."[42] CAPP points out that its stewardship program helps smaller companies by providing best practices guidelines for all producers, large and small.[43]

Alberta Energy Company, which merged with PanCanadian Energy to form EnCana in April 2002, won an award for environmental assessment at its Foster Creek project. Now the industry has a new subtrade of specialists doing environmental and Native relations work.

"Things are moving in a positive way. Companies do have to perform. There's an organized effort to find technical things companies can do that will clean up problems and areas where they can collaborate on environmental issues. The level of sensitivity on all sides is much higher than it used to be," adds Jaremko. "There's been a change in will."

That change has bulldozed some of the calcified layers within the industry that saw the landowner as simply an unnatural impediment to the thrust of the drill bit. The landmen—and now women—who search for land surface leases must press their negotiating skills into full diplomacy with farmers, ranchers, and other owners. This wasn't always the case.

"The landman is . . . a geologist or lawyer or both, otherwise a university graduate. He's a hustler, researcher, coddler, brain truster," states a 1964 article quoted in Shauna Kelly's book on the Canadian Association of Petroleum Landmen, called *Since It Began*.

"Land people are often at the forefront of projects, particularly when industry is dealing with the Aboriginal communities and development up North. We have the opportunity to go in and create a positive impression for all of industry because we truly are ambassadors in what we do," said one landman.[44]

Some farmers and ranchers may ask, "Ambassadors of what?" They worry about their animals grazing next to a gas-processing plant or downwind from a sour gas well that's accidentally flared.

Dr. Cheryl Waldner was concerned that a new sour gas processing plant at Caroline, in west-central Alberta, might have an
adverse effect on the animals she treated. As a veterinarian and
researcher, Dr. Waldner decided in 1991 to study the health of cattle in the region.

"Health indicators remained relatively consistent during this
period and within the range of values expected based on other
productivity and health surveys and suggested targets of performance," Dr. Waldner stated.[45]

Dr. Waldner continued her studies and in 1999 published her
doctoral thesis.

"She found a small, but significant, association between exposure to sour gas flaring from battery sites and the risk of stillbirth in
cattle. Less consistent associations were found with increased risk of
non-pregnancy, increased calving interval and calf mortality," wrote
Robert Bott, a highly respected veteran writer on the oil industry.[46]

Because there were some statistical but not proven linkages,
researchers, landowners, and the industry are paying attention.
The most ground-breaking study into the effects of industry emissions on animals began in November 2001 and will be completed
in 2004. The Western Interprovincial Scientific Studies Association
involves the four Western provinces and initially is examining
33,000 livestock, including 20,000 head of cattle. While the study
has the support of industry and governments, it is independent.

"The purpose of the study is to determine if exposure from oil
and gas emissions impacts animal and human health in Western
Canada," states Dr. Tee Guidotti, co-chair of the Science Advisory
Panel. "Previous research has not been conclusive, and this study
is different as it is more comprehensive both geographically and
in terms of the number of animal herds that are being studied.
This is an exciting project that applies world-class intellectual
resources to a challenging issue considered important by many
Western Canadians."[47]

The cost of the study is estimated to be $19 million and is currently funded by industry and the four Western Canadian provincial governments. The Science Advisory Panel consists of 10 renowned scientists in the fields of environmental and reproductive epidemiology, animal and human health, and toxicology. They will evaluate the methodology and science of the study to ensure the highest standards.

"This looks into a larger number of herds and animals, within a broader geographical area. It has scientific credibility and integrity. In the past, there's been inconsistencies in certain research procedures, such as post-mortems. We obviously need a sample size that's large enough to draw conclusions with statistical validity," says environmental scientist Michael O'Connell, the study manager.[48]

"We're building on some of the information that was garnered from previous studies. We're looking to make this a better study. We have a team of 10 renowned scientists that collectively reflect the goal of the study itself. A study of this magnitude has never been done. Industry clearly sees a need for a study of this issue."

O'Connell has noticed a sharp change in the industry's attitude toward the environment from the early 1980s, when "environmental issues were not high on the corporate agenda. Now it's up there. The environment is part of any company proposal."

That's why leading companies have encouraged synergy groups to form where they have large facilities. EnCana's Gwyn Morgan believes they're an important model for communication, discussion, and consensus.

"By and large, even in the Peace country, the former AEC was the first company to build a big gas plant there, and we set up a group that engaged everybody—the Saddle Hills Awareness Group," says Morgan, who pointed out that there are plenty of issues in addition to the environmental ones.

"It's not just the plant. What about the trucks on the roads? How are you going to maintain those roads? And what's it going to mean to the kids on the school bus? That whole idea of really proactive engagement has worked very well for us. We don't have any of our people on those groups, but they are working proactively with us."

One of the more visionary synergy groups is the Clean Air Renewable Energy coalition, which again brings the Pembina Institute into the forefront of progressive partnerships with industry. The purpose is to speed up economical renewable-energy industries through technological change and industry innovation.

"The Clean Air Renewable Energy coalition is working with the federal government to help devise tax incentives and other ways to support diversification of our energy supply, as well as to improve air quality and reduce emissions into the atmosphere," states Suncor CEO Rick George.

Another important synergy group is the Cumulative Environmental Management Association in Fort McMurray, which is doing exactly what its name suggests by pulling together all the stakeholders to examine the effects of multiple developments in the area. CEMA intends to bring its findings to government and industry.

One of the original partnerships between corporations and environmental groups is Alberta Ecotrust, which funds community programs that protect and improve the environment.

"It's an example of how it can work. People from industry sit around the table with community groups. It represents a vision for the future, one of cooperation, learning, and environmental achievement," says Peter Lougheed, former premier of Alberta and an honorary patron of the Ecotrust Foundation.[49]

As the petroleum industry spreads across the country into frozen tundra and churning oceans, synergy groups sprout to maintain environmental vigilance. The Sable Environmental Effects Monitoring Advisory Group includes Nova Scotia fisherman Charles Warner, who wants his way of life protected.

"We have a very viable fishery here. In order for the two industries to coexist, we have to work together," says Warner. "Monitoring is very important to the environment and people. We want the oil companies to do their homework. And by sharing information together, they learn from us, and we learn from them."[50]

For the first time, most of the 50 synergy groups working in Alberta's oil and natural gas areas had an opportunity to meet and discuss their challenges, successes, and strategies for change.

"Here were good people who believe the oil and gas industry is here to stay. They have to work with that and build relationships. It takes time. There's no cookie-cutter approach. They never make headlines [but] they solve problems," says Simone Marler, former manager of communications at CAPP. "They're still very wary of each other and they don't want to be co-opted. The pace of development has increased at such a rate. I think people are working hard, but for every good story, there's another person feeling frustrated."[51]

These groups do work hard for change. They've become very sophisticated and can stop a well even before it becomes a spark in a producer's arsenal. Their time and tenacity have been used to take the strongest companies to task, sending many a project prospect to the scrap heap. The influence and success of synergy groups show that they are a pivotal step in the industry's acceptance of environmental accountability.

"Shell Canada had a well rejected a year ago near Rocky Mountain House," says Gordon Jaremko. "Yet Burlington Resources got its well approved. Burlington went way out of its way, while Shell kind of took things for granted. The message is: Never take anything for granted. That's where the industry has to go. That whole area of Sundre–Caroline–Rocky Mountain House is the cradle of improved performance on the environment and nature."

This is due in no small measure to dedicated environmental activists like Martha Kostuch of Rocky Mountain House and the entire SPOG team in that area. The progress also owes much to the diligence of the Pembina Institute, and to environmentalists within the industry who make the extra effort to respect communities by communicating first. And lastly, credit must go to those industry leaders who have buried the old ways in the flare pits of the past.

CHAPTER FIVE

The Rules

If it smells, it stops. That's the first rule Neil McCrank insists that Alberta's petroleum industry follows no matter what it's doing and how much any delays might cost. The man at the top of the provincial enforcement derrick is fierce about his duty to protect the people and the environment where the industry operates.

"If it smells, we shut it down," says McCrank, who chairs the Alberta Energy and Utilities Board (EUB), the regulatory agency that oversees all oil and gas operations in the province.[1] The model for other such agencies in Canada, and sometimes a model for regulation in other countries, it is the last line of defence between an aggressive industry and the environment.

McCrank's manner is affable but his message is unmistakeable. His firm resolve is to ensure that the smell rule is the immovable rock before and during any development.

The second rule is: Communicate.

"It's a changed world," explains McCrank. "We have to be much more open and understanding of people's concerns. We still have companies who feel they have a God-given right to drill where they want. We still have people at our board who believe we don't have to explain things. I think we thought it was business as usual, but it wasn't. We're turning the corner, but we're not all there."

While McCrank is too discreet to say so, part of the problem was provincial cuts to the Board's budget during the mid-1990s, when a small-government advocate named Steve West reigned as Alberta's energy minister. At the same time as the Board was shrinking, the industry exploded with growth, leading to widespread fears that companies would be left unregulated.

Industry activity jumped dramatically during the 1990s, with a record-breaking number of wells drilled in 1994, 1996, 1997, and 2000–01. In the past three years, 35,800 new wells have been drilled in Alberta, nearly the same number (37,000) that were drilled in the 55 years from 1915 to 1970.[2]

Within the last 10 years, the EUB has seen its workload more than double, with total applications rising from 12,842 in 1990 to 25,544 in 1997 to 30,096 in 2000–01.[3]

Clearly, the EUB needed to be enhanced, not hacked, if it was to regulate the industry and protect people and the environment. Instead, the downsizing gave companies a classic opportunity to dodge around the rules. But responsible industry leaders, far from taking advantage of the Board's weakness, deplored it and lobbied the provincial government to restore the cash.

"I'd been pushing for more funding for them for quite some time," says EnCana CEO Gwyn Morgan.[4] Other industry leaders did the same, recognizing the danger to their reputation and the environment if companies, especially smaller ones, were left unregulated.

It finally worked. The EUB's budget for 2001–02 is $100 million, up from $57.4 million in 1994–95 and $54.9 million in 1995–96. (In 1939, the Board's forebear, the Petroleum and Natural Gas Conservation Board, had to make do with $33,850. The magic $1-million mark was hit in 1956–57.)

"There's no question. We lost a little bit in the mid-1990s and we're starting to gain that back," notes McCrank, diplomatically. "I don't think we recognized the changing public and the changing industry."

The first and most obvious change is a public that is more demanding, educated, and inquisitive. "Frankly, they're entitled to answers to their questions. In most cases it is their resource [which Albertans as a whole own through the Crown] and it is their environment. The public should have an interest in safety and health," says McCrank.

In the past, Board interventions over oil and gas developments were not common. Today, nothing goes through without the Board asking tough questions, and then getting the answers, before granting approvals.

But the EUB doesn't see itself as an enemy of the industry. Part of its job is to foster development that is both safe and expeditious. The industry demands timely decision-making, and if companies don't get it, says McCrank, "They'll take their money elsewhere, to a more responsive environment. Time is money in this fast world we live in."

The oilpatch is also clamouring for a more level playing field. Companies want to be treated consistently and fairly wherever they operate in the province.

"This is happening at a time when the industry is far different than it was years ago. In the 1970s we used to regulate about 60 companies, and today the total is well over a thousand," explains McCrank. "That's a whole different regulatory environment than used to exist."

Most of those early companies operated in remote bush, far removed from the buzz of the city. Today, with the province's dramatic increase in population and the urban flight to acreages and rural havens, the potential for conflict between landowners and the industry has escalated sharply. Applications for sour gas wells near major cities have raised tough resistance from worried residents. As people arm themselves with as much information as they can ingest, they insist on knowing exactly what any project entails, and what the risks are.

McCrank welcomes the questions. "Now we're far more open about what our role is and we try to educate the public," he says. "The public is far more involved through more than 50 synergy groups and we're encouraging that through our field offices."

These synergy groups, described in Chapter Four, bring together landowners, industry representatives, regulators, environmentalists, and any other interested parties before a project is formally proposed. Through its open houses, the Board presents itself as a conciliator between various stakeholders and the regulated petroleum industry.

"We go through a stakeholder process that is practically unparalleled," says EUB engineer Kim Eastlick. "We do a PEP for each community's needs."[5] In an industry overloaded with acronyms, PEP stands for something with real substance. The letters mean profile, educate, and propose. The old style was best described as DAD—decide, announce, and defend.

Once concerns are aired and potential problems debated, the project usually proceeds, but often with crucial amendments. Before the projects clear the substantial hurdles, companies prepare well and follow the rules—but not, as some critics say, because the EUB is somehow the industry's captive agency.

"Industry is more aware that its economic interest is to become more concerned about the public's issues," says McCrank. "Companies have developed stewardship programs. In fact, the program that CAPP [the Canadian Association of Petroleum Producers] has presented is fabulous and shows that they understand their responsibility.

"Some companies are very good corporate citizens and they would have participated in synergy groups in any case. For others, it's simply an economic solution to avoid conflict," says McCrank. "We talk to landowners and companies and try to get everyone together to solve problems. We've tried to become more of an instrument to settle conflicts."

The Board's Appropriate Dispute Resolution process is a good start. Its purpose is to present "a range of dispute resolution mechanisms" before or, in many cases, instead of a traditional hearing. While the ADR is voluntary, it has become a valuable tool for resolving conflicts before they fester and spoil relationships between companies and communities.[6]

"Companies must inform potentially impacted parties of the nature of the proposal or significant changes to operations, respond to questions and concerns, and seek understanding through collaborative efforts," states an EUB Informational Letter. "If disputes arise, the use of ADR should be considered."[7]

The ADR attempts to give local solutions to local problems through negotiation, facilitation, mediation, and arbitration. The EUB also points out that "parties do not lose any right they may have to a hearing by entering into ADR discussions."[8]

Anyone who has ever attended an EUB hearing knows that they can be long, laborious, and expensive. For those not trained as lawyers, the hearing is an alien and technical place. From everyone's perspective, it's more cost-effective to build relationships and goodwill rather than throw away cash to continue a conflict until winners and losers are declared.

The whole point of ADR is to help the major stakeholders develop acceptable solutions for a project instead of losing valuable time and resources. Conciliation, rather than confrontation, leads to negotiated decisions that are often more effective and efficient.

The process works. In 2000–01, there were 30,096 applications submitted to the EUB. Only 19 went to a contentious public hearing.[9]

Any project that reaches a public hearing usually has acrimony and even enmity behind it. But, ultimately, the project backers are likely to end up doing what would have been proposed during an ADR session anyway. There are three possible outcomes to an EUB hearing, and two of them are extremely unlikely: complete denial or blanket approval of a project exactly as presented.

The vast majority of projects are approved with a series of conditions that are designed to offset, meet, or mitigate the contentious issues. If a company doesn't comply, "The consequences are too severe to ignore," says Eastlick.

Ignoring EUB rulings can shut down a project or see it abandoned, with huge risk to the company's reputation, bank balance, and stock value.

"We don't run risks with companies," continues Eastlick. "We identify noncompliance issues, and if you choose to ignore us or there's some deliberate misconduct there, you run the risk of losing the entire operation."

The EUB issues "shut-in orders" every couple of weeks to stop noncomplying wells or facilities from operating. McCrank contends, correctly, that companies that follow the rules now enjoy a major competitive and economic advantage over firms that try to twist regulations for their own benefit.

Still, some experts are dubious about the pace of change, including Dr. Brian Bietz, a former member of the EUB. "The industry is slowly growing to realize that past practices are not acceptable," he says. "But [environmental responsibility] is not strong and proactive—they react. Few see it as economically beneficial—they see it as a cost."[10]

While Bietz believes too many in the industry see just the cost behind environmental regulations, he does acknowledge that some companies, and their chief executives, are guiding the industry by example.

"Gwyn Morgan at EnCana is a leader. So is Charlie Fischer at Nexen," says Bietz. "Eric Newell at Syncrude and Rick George at Suncor are also walking the talk."

Debbie Taras, an environmental consultant who has worked in the oilpatch for 20 years, is also concerned that money rules all environmental decisions.

"It's money versus the environment. Oil revenues keep this province growing at the expense of the environment," says Taras.

"If it smells, it isn't shut down necessarily. People out in the field are stretched to the limit, and all the companies want is approval, so the field people are pressured."[11]

Taras, an agrologist, believes the oilpatch is over-regulated in small things, with too little attention paid to large issues. There are a myriad of rules to be followed, especially the critical public consultations. "If you miss one little application that you didn't know you needed done, it can really push a project back. It's all very confusing." On the other hand, she worries that a lot of rubber-stamping occurs and would like to see the EUB's field force strengthened.

Martin Molyneaux, a highly regarded veteran analyst with investment banker FirstEnergy Capital, respects the work of the EUB, but sees room for improvements.

Regulation is "inadequate in some areas like reviewing wells that have discharges," he says. "The EUB is no longer viewed as an ombudsman with a foot in both camps. It's very much viewed in rural Alberta as being on the side of the producers. A decade ago that wasn't the case. It comes to funding and people."[12] McCrank counters that the Board has vastly increased its quota of field officers and they no longer drive in ghost cars and trucks. The vehicles are clearly marked to remind the industry and the public that the EUB is present.

He has some support from respected academic observers. "Despite the imagery of hard-driving entrepreneurs and free-enterprise politics which characterize the oil industry in the public mind, the industry in reality has functioned within the tight confines of a regulatory structure unmatched in any other resource sector," notes University of British Columbia history professor and author Dr. David Breen.[13]

The source of funding for the EUB is a serious issue. The industry and the provincial government used to contribute equally. That changed during the days of provincial government restraint in the mid '90s. Today the industry pays over 80 percent. Many observers complain that the EUB's dependence on industry funding erodes the board's independence and ultimately questions the legitimacy of its decisions. While the industry is highly supportive of the EUB's increased funding, many in the oilpatch would like to see the Alberta government return to its original sharing agreement of 50 per cent each. They argue that this would better reflect the public interest in EUB operations.

Some oilmen lament that they are over-regulated and powerless, even as environmentalists complain that the regulators are too soft. Among the former group is Al Markin, the affable chairman of Canadian Natural Resources. He and his wife, publisher Jackie Flanagan, are well-known for philanthropy in the cultural and social arenas.[14]

Markin insists that the relationship between the petroleum producers and the regulators is "not a democracy anymore. We're guilty until proven innocent. We're controlled now. We didn't use to be. The regulatory authorities are controlling."[15]

Not so, says one of the legends in the regulatory business. "It's a fine, delicate balance and one that's working," insists George Govier. "Of course the industry will always say it's over-regulated."[16] Govier was an engineer, scientist, university administrator, and professor who joined the Alberta Petroleum and Natural Gas Conservation Board in 1948 and acted as chairman from 1962 to 1978.

"It was a simpler time for the industry, which gets more complicated all the time," says Govier. "It's a different world than the one I knew." Govier is pleased about the re-funding of the EUB and the greater emphasis the Board has placed on the environment and public consultation.

"These are important efforts made by the Board to resolve issues before public hearings are required," he notes. "I was very concerned a number of years ago when budgets were cut and the

Board lost many of its talented people. A corner has been turned and I see the Board regaining its stature."

Former Alberta premier Peter Lougheed remembers the province's earlier environmental standards as multifaceted and dependent on strong regulators.

"We did a lot of things in terms of environmental control, as long as they were sensible, phased in, and recognized the costs," Lougheed notes. "The George Goviers of the world were strong and effective."[17]

As one of the country's most respected pioneer regulators, Govier is described by historian Breen as "remarkably energetic, disciplined and confident, [one who] expected the high standards that he set for himself to be met by those he supervised or with whom he worked."[18]

Govier believes those standards are more than being met by McCrank.

"I think the present chairman has a real talent for meeting people and solving problems before they get out of hand. That's very important," says Govier.[19]

McCrank sees one well-known regulation, EUB Guide 56, as more than the key conditions energy companies must meet before any project is green-lighted. Guide 56 also provides a measuring stick to skeptical citizens who may feel that the industry takes precedence over larger public interests.

"It maintains public confidence in the regulatory process. Companies must be proactive in their consultation with the public. We're shutting down operations on a daily basis for violation of regulations, but we haven't been telling people this," explains McCrank. "It's in everybody's interest, particularly the public, to know what we do."

The Canadian Association of Petroleum Producers once did an exercise to determine how many different departments, people, timelines, and information requirements were needed to get a project approved. Their "brown-paper" enterprise ended up being eight feet long.

"This was a significant revelation for us and the regulator. If only the public knew what industry has to go through to get an application approved," says CAPP vice-president David Pryce.[20] "There are significant and detailed expectations around the approval process."

And if the application involves a sour gas project, it is immediately classified as "non-routine." According to Pryce, the company must proceed through every hoop that can possibly be presented before the project is approved.

Whatever compromises are made, there is no fast track for sour gas, the natural gas that contains hydrogen sulphide. Sour gas is flammable, has a strong rotten-egg odour, and is poisonous to animals and humans. Although more than 97 per cent of the hydrogen sulphide is removed by gas-processing plants, the public, the industry, and the regulators are acutely aware of potential danger.

On December 18, 2000, the Advisory Committee on Public Safety and Sour Gas issued its exhaustive report, thick with 87 recommendations for improvements. It said: "The recommendations are generally directed towards increasing awareness of sour gas and its impacts on public health and safety, improving the sour gas regulatory system and encouraging better consultation that must take place with the public on all sour gas matters."[21]

McCrank says the blue-ribbon committee had a clear mandate to deal with issues and invited thorough and innovative stakeholder research. The progress of the recommendations is reported quarterly through EUB reports.

The public's main concern is health. People who live near sour gas wells want to know that they're safe and that companies have developed and can easily implement sophisticated emergency response plans. They also worry about the proliferation of wells, and how they're monitored and enforced. Above all, they want to be consulted and kept informed of any developments.[22]

Bietz believes that regulators must ensure that what they do makes sense for everybody. "It's a battle, and I see it in the environmental regulations. Companies just see a cost, not a benefit," he says. "There's a huge disconnect between the president's office and what happens in the field."

The bad companies sometimes tell operators in the field simply to cut costs, which can often mean a silent swathe past the path of environmental procedures. One company spread spills on its lease by simply incorporating the spill into the soil. "We have good record-keeping in case we ever get caught," the operator told an astonished Bietz. Another company told its operators that if they're ever shut down by the EUB, they're fired.

"How many CEOs have environmental benchmarks for their operators to which they attach bonuses, instead of telling them to minimize costs?" Bietz asks. (Several leading companies already do.)

Bietz is seeing some positive changes and insists the industry doesn't deserve to be pulverized over its relationship with the environment. For him, it's more an issue of benign neglect.

"In about '93, a hard-talking operator and I were out in the field. We were looking at a flare pit, and I asked him, 'Why do we still have these open ponds?' And he said, 'There's absolutely no reason.' It took some head-butting but we finally got the 'no more pits and ponds' through the EUB in the mid-'90s. There still are some.

"Any CEO worth his salt could have gone out and looked at all the stuff going into these sites and realized that sooner or later they would have to clean this up. The site cleanup is incredibly expensive. It's been like pulling teeth to get these guys to recognize the environmental costs."

Bietz admits the right CEO can change the company culture and the way things are done—or not done.

"The only reason we have any regulations at all is that the public wants them. Ultimately, that same public is your customer. They're the people you have to make happy. You'd think the company would buy into the fact that the happier the people are, the better we are. That is basic business."

But Bietz believes the oilpatch should be recognized for its initiatives in sustainability and sensitive environmental areas. He's delighted that they're saying to him "Tell us where we can't go, and then tell us where we can go."

The oilpatch has led the way in minimizing industry's footprint on the land, both in forested areas and on the prairies. By creating technological changes in seismic activity and drilling, the industry is able to lay seismic lines that are virtually invisible.[23]

Bietz is also impressed that the industry is taking a strong position on gas flaring in its research, and changing practices. "People are worried about emissions. That's a good place for them to focus," he says. "They're being reasonably proactive there."

The Clean Air Strategic Alliance (CASA) was instrumental in motivating industry to reduce gas flaring. Through debate, diplomacy, and consensus, CASA has now become the most effective of the numerous partnerships between industry, environmental nongovernmental agencies, the public, and government.

In 1998, CASA recommended a massive review of solution-gas management to reduce the volume of gas flared as well as to improve flare efficiency. (Solution gas is natural gas contained in crude oil.) All flares were examined to determine whether they could be eliminated or reduced. As a result, in 2002, a new EUB Guide 60 adopted the CASA framework for solution-gas venting, plant flaring, and well test flaring.

A document explaining the new guide says: "The guide defines economic evaluation criteria, and operators are required to conserve economic solution gas. That is, the reductions have resulted from identification of economic conservation opportunities rather than the imposition of mandatory reductions."[24]

This is an industry success story, with solution-gas flaring reduced by 53 per cent from 1.3 billion cubic metres in 1996.

Where flaring couldn't immediately be eliminated, practices changed and improved. The initial target, which was considered a stretch at the time, was 25 per cent for 2001. In 1999, the industry had already reduced solution-gas flaring by 30 per cent, then moved to 38 per cent in 2000.

"We didn't ask the industry to do something that wasn't economically viable," says Eastlick. "What proved to be the case is that the gas is worth conserving. The industry performed well beyond the targets set."[25]

"This is quite an accomplishment," says long-time environmental activist Martha Kostuch. "People and farmers working around those flares have noticed an improvement."[26] As a veterinarian, Kostuch saw the effects of air pollution on animal health and was delighted that declining emissions resulted in a parallel and positive effect on the animals in her care. Now an active member of CASA, Kostuch has the goal of the complete elimination of flares and a massive reduction in venting.

"Dialogue is ongoing, and we're seeing some tremendous results. CASA is very positive about the collaborative process," says Kostuch. "There's a role for confrontation and for collaboration. It's not either/or. I'm a supporter of all non-violent approaches. We've had very successful collaborations."

Now the EUB and CASA want the same impressive results for venting. With the support of CAPP and the Small Explorers and Producers Association of Canada, they're asking that venting be evaluated for the conservation of economic gas.

"Operators that report venting of solution gas are required to commence evaluation of gas conservation in 2002," says an EUB general bulletin to all oil and gas operators.[27] The study will be done in 2003 and will, at the discretion of the EUB, include an audit of certain operators.

Aging sour gas processing plants have also been targeted. Either they must meet current emission standards by 2016 or they're out of business. Again the industry is trying to meet the targets faster, with sulphur emissions from grandfathered facilities down by one-third of the 2016 goal. Their record for recovering sulphur has always been much stronger than that of coal-fired plants for generating electricity.

In general, sulphur emissions from larger sour gas plants are down significantly from 1970's 245,000 tonnes per year. By 2000, emissions had dropped dramatically to 78,000 tonnes, and even further, to 68,000 tonnes, in 2001.[28] And this improvement is occurring even though far more sour gas is produced.

"We have a number of success stories in addition to flaring and venting," says Gary Webster, formerly of CAPP. "Benzene from glycol dehydrators has been reduced by over 70 per cent between 1995 and the end of 2000."[29]

Because benzene is now recognized as a carcinogen, the industry seizes rather than releases the volatile organic compound. The glycol dehydrator captures the benzene while taking any water out of the natural gas.

"The whole way we're managing waste is a real success story," continues Webster. "We're trying to minimize the amount of waste we're generating through recycling and innovation."

Tom Marr-Laing continues to be concerned about the way the industry is dealing with oil field waste as well as other land issues. But he's impressed with the industry's action on flaring.

As the Pembina Institute's director of Energy Watch, Marr-Laing was worried when government reductions cut into the regulator's ability to do its job. Industry flaring became the flashpoint, but once money was restored to the EUB, flaring was reduced.

"I've been quite pleased by how impressive the EUB is with air emission issues. It's a 180-degree turnaround. The Board is playing a very progressive and in some cases aggressive role," says Marr-Laing. "That's refreshing to be occurring, where the Board says something that I was expected to say."[30]

Marr-Laing believes the Board was simply a facilitator in the past, but has now become an environmental proponent or advocate. He's delighted with Pembina's role in effecting the changes. "This gives us a perspective that there's a way to make progress. The successes in the province have been around air-quality issues. Those around land issues are much fewer."

The EUB's Upstream Petroleum Industry Flaring Report lauds the gas-flaring work of CASA: "As the report shows, industry has made considerable progress in reducing solution-gas flare volumes."[31]

But there's more to be done. The EUB put companies on notice that flaring and venting must continue to drop through further gas conservation: "However, this is partially offset by a recent increase in reported solution gas vented volumes, primarily at bitumen wells and batteries."[32]

Many point out that technological advances will soon allow companies to nearly, if not entirely, eliminate flaring, as well as to substantially reduce venting. McCrank and the EUB have put the industry on notice that this is an achievable goal.

That's just one reason why he balks at any suggestion that the industry and the regulators are in bed together.

"I absolutely reject that notion. We walk a fine line and have the interests of the public from a social, economic, and environmental view. There is no bias in what we do," he says vehemently.

McCrank notes that Alberta's regulatory board is much larger than any other such body in the country. He also points out that the Board must take a long-term view, since the decisions it makes are for generations into the future.

McCrank took the chairmanship of the Board after a distinguished career as Alberta's deputy minister of justice. He's widely respected by experts such as Patricia Gariepy Leeson, a lawyer with the Alberta Securities Commission, who previously drafted the environmental regulations of the Environmental Protection and Enhancement Act.

"This is a man who is extremely capable and committed. He is also a man who is open, warm, and concerned about people," she says of McCrank. "He's very involved in his charities and very engaged in his community."[33]

As an electrical engineer as well as a lawyer, McCrank likes to say that "it helps to wear an iron ring and to have the legal training." That certainly gets him started after his one coffee in the morning, but his most crucial skill in these changing times is his ability to conciliate as well as communicate.

"The most important thing for the Board is to have highly qualified technical people that are the equal of those in industry," he says. "The public expects and deserves the confidence that their needs and interests are being met and that they are well-informed."

During the cutbacks, the industry scooped up many Board regulators, revelling in their technical expertise and regulatory know-how. While the Board's local reputation waned somewhat, its global standing remained high. Delegations from Australia, China, Poland, Kazakhstan, Korea, Mexico, Nigeria, Abu Dhabi, and Bangladesh have visited the Board over the past few years to find out how the regulatory process is supposed to work.

"We haven't promoted that with the public," says McCrank. "It's a difficult process bridging the gap between perception and reality. All we have to do is bridge that gap."

McCrank's supporters within the industry believe the EUB is doing important work. "I think Neil McCrank and his team have really got a forward-looking approach. They're very responsible and they've really focused their efforts on mediation," says Gwyn Morgan.

One of the industry achievements is the Orphan Well Fund. In the early 1990s, people were concerned about problem well sites that were simply left by previous owners. Often, no one was responsible for cleaning them up.

The United States tried a method called "Super Fund Sites," making anyone with a remote connection to a well responsible for its cleanup. The outcome was predictable—perennial legal battles and putrid sites that often festered for many years before the disputes were resolved.

In Alberta, the regulator was watching and wondering how to protect the public and the environment from a growing number of abandoned wells. In 1993, the industry created an insurance fund and came up with the orphan well program.

There were some initial shortcomings, since the fund focused only on orphaned wells. When the industry first got going in Alberta, a company would drill, produce the well until it became uneconomic, and then simply leave it. "There wasn't too much thought going into what to do to the soil," says David Pryce.

That was the mentality going into the 1950s and '60s. Once the level of activity dramatically rose, so did environmental concerns. Landowners clamoured to have the sites cleaned up.

Recently the reclamation of sites has been very positive, with 90 per cent of industry reclamation certificates approved, up from 65 per cent in 1996.[34]

"Now we have an orphaned facilities program that will pay for the cleanup of wells and batteries as well as reclamation and remediation," says Pryce. "Today there is a mechanism where, if there is an unfunded liability, the EUB will manage and do the cleanup on behalf of the producers."

"The producers collectively and voluntarily pay for this work," he adds. "We don't want the public or the landowner to be out of pocket. Not many, if any, other industries take on this kind of responsibility."

The EUB's stated mission is to ensure that the discovery, development, and delivery of Alberta's resources take place in a manner that is fair, responsible, and in the public interest. Its vision is to continue to build a regulatory framework that inspires public confidence. This is achieved through values that focus on fairness, competence, and quality. The EUB core businesses are applications;

adjudication and regulation; surveillance and enforcement; and information and knowledge.

"We were very much like the Texas Railroad Commission. It was the granddaddy of them all and we were designed after them," says McCrank.

The Texas Railroad Commission, which didn't change its name, initially had some responsibility for the railroads, but now looks after all the oil and gas in Texas.

The commission was established in part "to protect the vested rights" of small producers. Breen is quick to criticize those who see the Board "as the centrepiece of a regulatory framework that was adopted uncritically from the practice in the U.S. oil-producing states that they believe fostered the interests of the large oil companies."[35]

Instead, says Breen, "Texas regulatory practice, which is usually cited as the model for Alberta legislation, was in fact geared more towards protecting the interests of the smaller independent Western-based oil companies."[36]

While the Texas Railroad Commission doesn't have an environmental mandate, the EUB certainly does, along with the Alberta government. Given the overlap, McCrank wonders whether anything might be falling through the cracks in regulating the industry.

"Maybe we might administer the environmental regulations so that there is only one body responsible," he says. "Government makes the rules but we administer the environmental regulations."

Ever since the E. coli tragedy in Walkerton, Ontario, water use and water quality have emerged as major public concerns. There is a water allocation policy that clearly states the industry must use the least-drinkable water, which is found in deeper wells, provided that it is available and economically viable to use. Yet current techniques such as enhanced oil-recovery methods need large amounts of water. Any surface water that is used in enhanced recovery must be in line with the Water Act, which means obtaining a water licence through Alberta Environment. Producers hold only about 2.5 per cent of the licences issued in the province, and they use only 40 to 60 per cent of their allocation. David Pryce refers to a recent independent study done for CAPP that overturns the idea that producers are water culprits and confirms "that removing the quantity of water desired from the source of supply can be done without unreasonably impacting the source of supply, the rights of household users, traditional agricultural users, and prior licencees or the environment in general."[37]

There have been important advantages to the petroleum industry's search for water. A vast amount of data is required to obtain and maintain an industry water licence. That data is stored and is available to the public, so all who live nearby are able to use the information to help determine where to drill their own wells or otherwise locate water for their needs.

The CAPP study concluded that current public concerns over the use of water by the upstream oil and gas industry are unwarranted.

"It seems unlikely that the use of surface water for enhanced recovery significantly impacts irrigation by precluding its availability for irrigation," the report states. "It seems unlikely that the agriculture community and household users in rural residential subdivisions would be negatively affected."[38]

Environmentalists like Tom Marr-Laing want more assurances. He continues to worry about land and water pollution, and wonders how oilfield waste is being managed and what its impact is on agricultural land. "It gets back to the practices of the best companies versus the worst," he says.

In the end, the only reason for regulations is to protect the public. The rules are not designed to protect the companies, but rather to safeguard public values and health.

Eastlick sympathizes with CEOs who feel the industry is over-regulated, but the EUB also has to deal with a wide diversity of capability and sophistication among more than 1,200 oilpatch companies in the province.

"There are also cases of operators who don't know what they don't know. They need some understanding of the issues," he says. "We need a regulatory backstop so we can take action on issues."

Eastlick explains that, to a large extent, the regulatory systems have been designed for project-by-project decisions. When there's massive development in an area such as Fort McMurray, regulators need to worry about the cumulative effects, such as quality of air and pollution of land, as well as societal changes. The huge amount of drilling activity has been a challenge for regulators.

"It calls for a different mindset, and we have to manage all of that fairly," says Eastlick. "It's a matter of knowing what we can tolerate."

Regulators expect that criticism of sour gas developments will continue to rise, given the growing number of those projects in the works in Alberta, Saskatchewan, and British Columbia. Currently, one-third of Alberta's natural gas production is sour gas. "H_2S is a dangerous substance and there should be criticism," says Eastlick.

He insists that Alberta's environmental standards are sufficient to handle sour gas developments. Certainly Alberta's ambient air–quality standards are among the most stringent in North America, and Alberta Environment continues to enhance its provincial standards.

Aboriginal peoples have used the environmental standards and upgraded regulatory procedures to ensure their communities are number one when a project is proposed on or near their lands. "There's a whole corps of experts doing this now in the industry and in the Aboriginal communities who are intermediaries between the two," says Jerome Slavik, lawyer and veteran land claims expert. "This is to head off any disputes over environmental issues and social and economic benefits."[39]

In March 2002, the National Energy Board issued a memorandum of guidance explaining that the Crown has a fiduciary obligation to Aboriginal people when decisions or actions have the effect of interfering with Aboriginal or treaty rights. The NEB's role is to ensure that adequate Crown consultation takes place, potential impacts are discussed, and remediation is proposed. To that end, the NEB asks applicants to consult with Aboriginal people over any project that is planned in their area, and then to file information from those consultations with the Board. It is beyond the constitutional power of any province to infringe upon Aboriginal rights or title. For its part, the Canadian Association of Petroleum Producers has informed its members of recent court decisions and pointed out that each step in the regulatory approval process must comply with the legal obligation to consult. When Aboriginal title is infringed, equitable compensation is compulsory.[40]

The industry has taken a dramatic turn in its relations with Aboriginal peoples, who found ways to effectively delay or stop approval of projects by hiring lawyers and scientists to substantiate their environmental and land claims positions.

"The difference between a contested and uncontested hearing can be anything from $10 million to $50 million," notes Slavik. That's a massive addition to any project with the regulatory board as bait.

In 1990, in a landmark decision, the Supreme Court of Canada ruled that Section 35 of the Constitution Act of 1982 provides "a strong measure of protection for Aboriginal rights. Any proposed regulations that infringe on the exercise of those rights must be justified." The case became known as the *Sparrow* case, after Ronald Sparrow, a Musqueam Native, appealed his conviction for fishing in the lower Fraser River with a longer-than-permitted driftnet.[41]

The *Sparrow* decision proved that governments have an obligation to consult with Aboriginal peoples when any government policies and decisions are going to affect treaties and Aboriginal rights. "Any activity of licensing that affects hunting and trapping triggers that requirement to consult, because it interferes with treaty-protected rights," adds Slavik. "It may seem like a flimsy excuse, but from a legal point of view it's right."

Much has changed in the oil industry over the past 25 years. Through this change, the science of oil and gas exploration has been elevated to a level that is incomparable in the world.

"The oil industry in Alberta has been blessed by the regulatory authority," says Wilf Gobert, long-time analyst at investment banker Peters & Co. "The ability to do research here is the best in the world. The provincial lab is housed in the EUB."[42]

Companies are required to donate drilling cores to the laboratory, which has become a crucial research house for anyone in the oilpatch.

"Progressive regulations caused individual companies to develop better technology that is less invasive to the land," adds Gobert, citing portable seismic, GPS, and directional drilling. "There's vibro-seis for seismic shooting versus setting off charges in the past." Where possible, companies now use vibrating machines instead of blasts that set the earth vibrating.

Regulatory authorities can also take credit for some massive technological changes in the oilsands. With the reclamation of mine sites requiring restoration of the surface, when it's completed, it's hard to tell that mining operations ever existed on the sites. Of course, current operations are acutely obvious with their huge footprints, but those sites will also be restored when they're mined out. "It will all be invisible to the naked eye one day," adds Gobert.

The Pembina's Tom Marr-Laing focuses on another regulatory challenge. He's pleased with the flaring results, but would like them increased to 80 per cent reduction (from 53 per cent) over the next few years. "What nobody knows is where the line is between the economic and the non-economic reduction," says Marr-Laing. "There's no downside in terms of return on investment now."

He wants to know the point at which the reductions actually cost the company money and, from there, what is the public role. Reduced pollution becomes an environmental plus in which the public shares.

"Is it fair to have some kind of cost-sharing?" he wonders. "As long as a company can do that and not lose money, then the company should do that. But when it starts to lose money, then the public should play a role. So, how much money are the government and the public willing to pay?"

CAPP's David Pryce points out that all the flaring gas can be used, even though the industry and the Crown view it as waste.

"For economic reasons, if we decided we would collect that waste gas at an added expense, it would be costly because we would have to pay royalties on it," says Pryce. Now the Crown has said it will waive the royalties if the industry can prove that collecting the gas is uneconomic.

"That did get the industry thinking, and it's looking at collecting some of the uneconomic gas that's flared. We won't have to pay royalties, yet it is good for the environment," he adds.

Of course, on a hard economic basis, if a company spends $100,000 and is not making any money from the gas saved from flaring, the project doesn't make much sense. But from a public relations perspective, the spending creates a great amount of goodwill.

"The analogy I use is that of a rubber band. The rubber band connects public expectations and actions being taken by government and industry," Marr-Laing says. "Through the '90s, that rubber band got stretched to the upper level. Flaring became the flashpoint with reductions in government monies to regulators." But Marr-Laing believes that the government and industry have moved in the right direction, in large part because of public pressure.

"They're taking direction to close the gap on what the public expects them to do," he says. "I hope to not be in a situation where industry rests on its laurels. My view is that the credibility relationship is a moving target for both sides."

The industry certainly realizes that a number of flashpoints continue as companies explore and drill in new areas while population expands into the country as well as in the city.

"The CEOs don't want to leave a mess. They're environmentalists too," says Peter Lougheed, who knows a good number of them, and who has probably spent more time hiking in the Alberta bush and mountains than those who criticize the industry. He too considers himself an environmentalist.

Environmentalists—and they are very much within the industry as well as outside—would like to see an absolute limit placed on the pace of development, with the EUB playing an ever more prominent role.

All of this is ultimately embedded in the psychic capital of the entire province. The industry and government must recognize the limits to growth and the policy framework that is required to contain the best in sustainable development.

"I remain hopeful, because there have been good changes. It can be done and the tools are there," adds Marr-Laing. "It is a question of conscience, and psychic capital."

Alberta Union of Provincial Employees president Dan MacLennan feels that other industries can learn from the best practices of the oilpatch.

"Years ago, the flat denial on flaring was a concern. Now that's all changed with pressure from the public," says MacLennan. "I think it's unfortunate that other industries, like feedlots and hog farms, haven't learned from these guys. Those organizations are a decade behind the oilpatch."[43]

MacLennan has only praise for McCrank and the EUB. "I like Neil McCrank," he offers. "And if everyone's mad at them at the same time, they're doing a good job."

Oilweek editor Gordon Jaremko says, "The fact of life is that for competitive reasons companies will do only what everybody else is deemed to be required to do."[44]

Jaremko doesn't feel that regulations were any more relaxed in the past, but their enforcement is more rigorous today. That, he believes, is due to politics and public pressure. "A lot of people don't think the oil and gas industry is the goose that laid the golden egg.

They think of it as the vulture scraping away the beauty of the land. And they will act on that with vigilance," he says.

In March 2000, Jaremko interpreted the role of the EUB as "a true friend" of both industry and the public.

"Captains of industry can lower their blood pressures, and improve their prospects, if they learn better than to deride government requirements as red tape. Public consultation, hearings, conditions on project approvals and even occasional rejections are the products of friends at work—not natural enemies," wrote Jaremko.[45]

Suncor chief executive Rick George believes that companies that are open and willing to talk, listen, and make changes end up with positive experiences.

"For us, it has probably meant less of a confrontational regulatory process and more of a collaborative one," he notes.[46]

As EnCana's CEO, Gwyn Morgan is one of the most respected and influential oilmen in the country. He welcomes the changing role of the industry and the regulatory authorities.

"Obviously, from a technical point of view, it's not as if we've suddenly changed our environmental practices. This industry has been improving steadily for years and years. I would put our record up against any industry of any kind anywhere," he says.

Morgan points out that it's difficult to separate social and technical issues.

"The social issues are in some ways part of the technical issues. Where we need to get better is how we relate to communities. I think that's something more enlightened people are working on and realizing that the EUB is doing a good job. None of us is perfect, and we're all going to have our problems, and once in a while, we're going to have some kind of unexpected thing happen. I think overall we're making some pretty good progress as an industry."

The Tools

The call came an hour before midnight. It was a potential Stage 3 full-scale emergency at a sour gas well, which meant that control of the well could be lost. The scene was the "war room" of a Calgary-headquartered oil and gas company. This was a critical situation, but there was no pandemonium, no barking of orders—just focused attention to the serious task at hand. Every person in the room had a clearly defined job, and the communication between those at the problem well and those in the room was instantaneous and continuous. The emergency response plan was in place, and the well specialists and engineers were working furiously to quickly contain the leak.

The safety of the workers at the site was assured as they continued their task to completely contain the well. Company officials had contacted residents, the Alberta Energy and Utilities Board, the RCMP, and county administrators and had a helicopter standing by. An emergency centre was established and residents immediately downwind of the well were evacuated, as was a group of hunters. Air-monitoring equipment was activated, and roadblocks, complete with crew, were set up. Weather forecasts were monitored for any potential change in wind direction and velocity.

Each precious minute was fuelled by anticipation as the drill crew quickly searched for, found, and then fixed the source of the leak. The mood in the "war room" lifted as the scale of the emergency fell. The danger was now over, and the "war room" itself seemed to contract in relief. The monitoring would continue, and the post-mortem meetings on the emergency and the response would be examined in detail, with changes instituted immediately—or else.

I witnessed this scene in the Calgary offices of a major integrated oil company. It was in no way unusual: Such tense, quiet dramas might play out in any petroleum company with sour gas wells. The emergency could come once a year or once a decade. But when there is any kind of leak at a sour gas well or facility, the company's emergency response plan springs into action. It had better be effective and efficient unless the company wants the regulators, the media, and the public on its case.

Things have changed dramatically since the infamous 1982 Lodgepole incident in central Alberta. An Amoco Canada high-pressure sour gas well blew out of control and burned for 68 days, killing two seasoned well-capping specialists from Texas. Sixteen others landed in the hospital, and the rotten-egg smell wafted as far as Winnipeg. Its repercussions remain with us today.

"The incident spawned a new generation of safety regulations, requiring the industry to designate hazardous drilling targets as 'critical wells' and to accompany the drilling with elaborate safety precautions," wrote Peter McKenzie-Brown, Gordon Jaremko, and David Finch.[1]

Ever since Lodgepole, companies wanting to drill in sour gas areas could find themselves at the centre of controversial regulatory hearings. Reminding everyone how important the industry is to jobs and government coffers is not the way to quell a concerned public that insists on the utmost safety assurances. That's why the Alberta Energy and Utilities Board has strict guidelines on critical sour gas projects and insists on very specific and detailed public consultation. The Oil and Gas Commission of B.C. also follows similar procedures.

"Critical sour gas wells are those with the potential for large H_2S releases or for any release that can affect population centres," writes Robert Bott. "In designating critical sour gas wells, regulators also consider population density, the environment, the sensitivity of the area and the expected complexities during the drilling phase."[2]

Armed with more staff and the authority to fine and even shut down company operations, regulators work to respond quickly and effectively to stakeholders' complaints, whether the concerns are about pollution in the air, the land, or the water.

Energy companies are required to file emergency response plans with the authorities that regulate sour gas facilities and critical sour gas wells. There are strict criteria to ensure the safety of all who live or work near sour gas operations. Each company's emergency response plan explains how people within the planning zone will be contacted and, if need be, evacuated. The zone can extend for more than 10 kilometres, depending on the absolute open flow of the well, or maximum potential release volumes for a pipeline. When a well being drilled approaches a likely sour gas spot, residents in the zone are immediately contacted.[3]

In addition to a comprehensive emergency response plan, Bott points out other crucial safeguards that must be met before a sour gas well can be drilled. Detailed drilling plans and procedures, including the precise design of the well, must be submitted. Regulators want to know that experienced safety specialists are on the scene and that workers and their supervisors are proficient in sour gas awareness and procedures. Regulators also ensure that the technology is up to date and there's "equipment such as blowout preventers, mud-gas separators, drill pipe and valves."[4]

Sour gas can kill. It's a colourless natural gas that contains hydrogen sulphide (H_2S), which is toxic and flammable. At low concentrations, sour gas smells like rotten eggs. At mid-level concentrations, it kills the sense of smell, while at higher levels, it's lethal.

Because it's heavier than air, hydrogen sulphide will tend to flow into low-lying areas such as ditches and trenches. It can rise, however, if it becomes warmer than the surrounding air. Finally, if hydrogen sulphide is under pressure, it can travel with ferocity in any direction it can find. Canada's natural gas production is one-third sour gas, which comes mainly from Alberta and northeast British Columbia. Sour gas is also found in sewers, septic tanks, stockyards, and underground mines.[5]

People can smell H_2S at concentrations of less than one part per million (ppm). The Clean Air Act air-quality standard in Alberta for one hour is 0.01 ppm. At 10 ppm, the odour is clearly offensive and can cause the eyes to water and swell. At this concentration, workers can stay at the site for no more than eight hours. At concentrations above that, the site will be evacuated. The concentration maximum varies across the country, with Alberta, British Columbia, and Quebec at the lowest end of the scale at 10 ppm and Nova Scotia at the highest with 30 ppm, followed by Ontario and Newfoundland at 20 ppm. The federal limit is 11 ppm.

At 100 ppm, H_2S kills the sense of smell. At 500 ppm, sour gas attacks the nervous system, causing the victim to lose balance and reasoning. The victim is knocked out at 700 ppm, and at 1,000 ppm, the victim dies or is permanently brain-damaged, unless there is an immediate rescue.

Energy companies are acutely aware of the dangers of sour gas, and employees working at or near such facilities are trained to recognize, report, and respond to any emergency. They know they have an immediate responsibility to fellow employees and people who live near the site. All sour gas sites have detectors that monitor H_2S levels, as do people who work with sour gas.

"The most widely recognized training program for sour gas workers is the one-day 'H$_2$S Alive' course offered by the Petroleum

Industry Training Service [PITS], through a network of more than four hundred PITS-certified instructors," explains Bott.[6]

Oilweek magazine points out that safety standards and training are so sophisticated in Canada's oilpatch that they're "in demand in more than 30 countries." The best is the one mentioned by Bott. PITS is a collective non-profit company, supported by industry and government, that has developed more than 100 courses and certified more than 80,000 workers around the world.[7]

Oilfield safety has advanced dramatically since the days when companies refused to pay for courses, and employees had to meet off-hours to learn what to do in emergency situations. Accidents were part of the job.

"But still, safety cannot be said to have been company policy," writes Fred Stenson, describing the late 1940s. "The men were responsible for their own safety, their own safety meetings, their own safety programs; with the company kicking in some cash when needed to make a change. Although credit should be given to these early superintendents, foremen and operators for having the wisdom to work towards making their plants safe, it must also be recognized that knowledge of the hazards was lacking in this era."[8]

No longer. An important field in the petroleum industry is health and safety, with a myriad of companies developing products, offering courses, devising innovations, and generating technologies to make the work site and the surrounding area safer. When the oil and gas companies caught the safety wave, they rode it into a change of attitude. The best companies are proud of their health and safety record but are quick to point to necessary improvements.

"Safety is an area where things are quite different. The level of sensitivity on all sides is much higher than where it used to be. It's a change in will," observes *Oilweek* editor Gordon Jaremko.[9]

In 2000, the EUB created a sour gas advisory committee that came up with 87 recommendations designed to improve public safety concerning sour gas issues. By 2003, all the recommendations will be carried out, with 46 well under way at the end of 2001. Oil and gas producers identified four important initiatives: more effective emergency response plans; increased EUB inspections and audits; more inclusive and productive public consultation; and the "highest priority response to sour gas complaints."

"The petroleum industry needed to listen to the people living near these operations. The public needed to know that the industry and the regulator were ready to act," noted Frank George, an industry representative involved in the EUB review.[10]

Nonetheless, so little hydrogen sulphide escapes into the atmosphere that there are no figures on the amount emitted by the industry. Most H_2S in sour gas is processed into elemental sulphur, which is made into everyday products such as pharmaceuticals and fertilizers. The remainder is flared to break it down into water and sulphur dioxide (SO_2).

Like H_2S, sulphur dioxide is colourless, toxic, and heavier than air, but rises and dissipates rapidly into the air when burned. Sulphur dioxide smells like a burning match and becomes almost unbreathable because it is such an irritant to the respiratory tract.

The odour threshold for sulphur dioxide is anywhere between 1 and 3 parts per million, with 2 ppm being the eight-hour occupational exposure limit. The 15-minute exposure limit is 5 ppm. The eyes, nose, and throat become irritated between 8 and 12 ppm. There's an immediate danger to life at 100 ppm. The Alberta and British Columbia limit for one-hour ambient air quality is 172 parts per billion—that is, an hour is the maximum a worker can be exposed to that amount.

Far less of these toxins escapes today than in the early days of the industry. Sulphur recovery at sour gas plants has increased to nearly 99 per cent from 94 per cent in 1970, and newer plants recapture 99.8 per cent. Total sulphur emissions have dropped by 68 per cent in the same period. Thanks to technological advances and other innovations, total emissions of SO_2 have declined even as gas production has risen substantially.

"Industry performance has improved significantly," writes Melanie Collison about sulphur emissions and hydrogen sulphide recovery. "But even 99 percent is different than perfection, especially when the material involved is handled in such big quantities that the last one percent still has to be measured in tonnes."[11]

Producers were prodded in the past, but leaders from within their own community are now goading their brothers and sisters to become green. They're working with regulators and stakeholders like the Clean Air Strategic Alliance, developing measurable targets and achievable goals. The oilpatch is also actively monitoring and reducing emissions that contribute to greenhouse gases.

Greenhouse gases trap heat in the atmosphere, causing the earth to warm. While this is a natural occurrence that is essential to life, some human-produced gases appear to accelerate the greenhouse effect. Water vapour makes up 60 per cent of the greenhouse effect, while carbon dioxide (CO_2), nitrous oxide (N_2O), methane, chlorofluorocarbons, and others produce the rest.

Many believe humans are directly responsible for increasing the greenhouse effect; consequently, reducing greenhouse-gas emissions is a major priority for the petroleum industry. Any kind of responsible sustainable practice must include reducing emissions. It means cleaner air and, for the bottom-liners, a cleaner balance sheet, since using less energy ultimately costs less money.

The Clean Air Strategic Alliance, the partnership between industry, government, and non-governmental organizations, has this as one of its goals: "The air will be odourless, tasteless, look clear and have no measurable short- or long-term adverse effects on people, animals or the environment."[12]

The oil and gas industry planned to reduce routine solution-gas flaring voluntarily, but agreed to regulatory measures if targets weren't achieved. The CASA team also called for a report in 2002 to determine if the voluntary approach was proceeding and to evaluate the need for future targets. The industry agreed to cut emissions by 15 per cent for 2000, and 25 per cent for 2001.

The industry climbed on board voluntarily and successfully reduced flaring by 38 per cent for 2000, and a phenomenal 53 per cent for 2001. Now the target is even further reductions, with the industry goal of improving its operations while protecting the environment and preventing pollution.

"In September 2000, CASA set up a multi-stakeholder team at the request of the Alberta Energy and Utilities Board to review this progress, additional flaring from other facilities, and well test flaring and venting," says John Squarek, a manager with CAPP. "The project team will include recommendations to reduce venting as well as facility and well test flaring, and will recommend a review in 2003 on these matters."[13]

In 1995, Environment Canada formed the Working Group on Benzene Emissions from Glycol Dehydrators, with representation from industry, government, and environmental organizations.

"Even though the oil and gas industry makes a relatively small contribution to the total exposure to benzene, it recognized the importance of reducing benzene emissions, particularly in situations where the general public or workers could be exposed," explains Squarek.

Again, the working group decided a voluntary program would be the most effective way to address the issue. They were right. By January 2001, benzene emissions had dropped by 75 per cent from 1995 levels, and the goal for 2005 is 90 per cent.

The shift in attitude and awareness within the petroleum industry has been dramatic. Changes in technology have accelerated research and solutions to critical environmental problems. The industry hires and now listens to environmental scientists within its ranks, because most know that the issues raised must be resolved through cooperation rather than confrontation.

Flaring, venting, and sour gas and benzene emissions are issues that stare back at corporate executives as they face board members wanting solutions. Whether they like it or not, the boards of directors of today's large energy companies must buy into environmental health and safety innovations and research. The reason is simple: If the executive's conscience isn't troubled by faulty environmental practices, the company's bottom line certainly will be.

In the 21st century, shareholder value means much more than cash flow and earnings. There's an ethical component that can crush the company's profit, as the dramatic implosion of Enron and Arthur Andersen proves. Energy companies need to develop and adopt the most innovative technological practices available. Industry environmentalists who toil in the towers work tirelessly to change the mindsets of certain CEOs who balk at their colleagues who push greener practices.

The green CEOs also press the slackers to embrace the newer science and attitude. "We have the ability to drill wells now with very little impact," notes EnCana CEO Gwyn Morgan. "We've come a huge distance."[14]

That distance was too often littered with seismic lines, piercing noise, cut forests, and felled dreams of landowners living nearby. Today's new directional drilling systems can drop multiple wells from one drilling pad, leaving the rest of the land free from numerous and unsightly exploratory wells. The wells are slanted or curved so they can extend around or under sensitive areas in their search for petroleum. Drilling bits and rigs are more sophisticated, as are the drilling fluids, or "muds," which are now nontoxic. Well leases can also be much smaller (although they still must be big enough to ensure safe spacing for equipment and quick escape routes in case of emergency). All these innovations cut exploration time and environmental damage.

The old seismic practice of driving the Caterpillar through the forest, cutting and flailing at everything in its path, is gone, replaced by much narrower cutlines. Hand-cut seismic is often used, where crews with chainsaws walk into the forest and cut a narrow path. This clears the way for the heli-seismic operation, where a global positioning system (GPS) from within the helicopter gathers data that determines the location for drilling. The only impact of this system is transitory noise from the chopper. Packhorses have also been brought in to transport equipment, thus eliminating the need to cut vegetation.

"There's a gradation of seismic possibilities depending on the sensitivities," says CAPP vice-president David Pryce. "We assess each system on its merits, and there's technology for any kind of seismic."[15]

Today's seismic crews are able to shoot three-dimensional images that allow the producer much more sophisticated understanding of where to find the oil and gas. High-speed data processing, multi-channel digital recordings, and innovative computer technologies give producers the exploratory edge as they map out the formations that fuel successful discoveries.

Producers drilling exploratory wells no longer need to dig a sump into the ground. With sumpless drilling and "closed loop" systems, all the waste and fluids remain in the contained tank, where the cuttings are cleaned out and the fluids are recycled into the well. The muds remain in the tank and away from the groundwater. This process also uses far less water to drill the well.

Drilling rigs and bits are more environmentally friendly, using less energy, thus reducing greenhouse-gas emissions. Industry trucks and other services also use far less fuel.

"If tests indicate the well is a dry hole, not capable of producing commercial quantities of oil and gas, the drilling crew plugs the well bore with cement and cleans up the site. A similar procedure is followed if a producing well is no longer economical to operate," states Bott.

"Because of stringent environmental regulations, the cost of abandonment and cleanup is a significant factor in an oil company's planning. The company remains responsible for the site until a reclamation certificate is issued by government authorities."[16]

Industry has also taken the collective initiative to clean up old wells that were "orphaned" after their irresponsible bankrupt owners ditched them with all the mess.

"We bear the brunt of the legacy of those that have abandoned mines and not reclaimed them. The industry, through CAPP, is being proactive with the Orphan Well Fund and cleaning up after the fact," explains Syncrude CEO Eric Newell.

"The whole reclamation side gets at the issue of abandoned mines not being reclaimed. We returned the environment to a good productive state. We don't want to leave the impression that industry was negligent," notes Newell.[17]

New technologies in mining and upgrading the bitumen have sliced costs and made the Fort McMurray area deposits a profitable proposition. About $86 billion worth of investments have been announced for the oilsands over the next number of years. Newell and his colleagues like Suncor CEO Rick George are acutely aware of the technical challenges in extracting oil from the gooey tar sands.

They've worked to improve the air quality in the area over what it was five years ago. But they agree that's not enough. They also want to see a further drop in sulphur dioxide emissions from the upgraders. That's a start. Even though Syncrude has doubled its production over the last decade, it's seen an absolute reduction in SO_2 and a 75 per cent drop per barrel of the emission.

Syncrude is also working with manufacturers to get more efficient engines for the trucks, and Newell is concerned about reclamation.

"We are disturbing a lot of land, but the amount of disturbed land will go up much more and that will become an emerging issue. It will be reclaimed, but it is a challenge. Another area is water management. We take water out of the river and have reclaimed 80 per cent of the water we use. But it will become a challenge for us," explains Newell.

"The oilsands industry has a fantastic record in improving energy efficiency and reducing greenhouse gas. On a per barrel basis, the industry will reduce greenhouse-gas emissions by 45 per cent—that is 2 per cent efficiency per year, when the standard is 1 per cent reduction."

Since oilsands production has risen dramatically, greenhouse gases have gone up, but at a far slower rate. Greenhouse-gas production results from combustion. The better the technology, the more efficient the energy use and the lower the emissions.

"Syncrude has developed low-energy extraction. We produce a barrel of bitumen for 40 per cent less energy than we did five years ago. The technology and other new methods are a great source of improvement. That will continue," says Newell. "Over the long haul, we want to continue to reduce the energy intensity of the production processes. In the long run we will need every form of energy we can get."

Newell wants to see more money spent on research and development of alternative energy sources such as fuel cells and hydrogen. Alberta is also home to low-sulphur coal, which has the capacity to be environmentally friendly, unlike its high-sulphur–burning cousins in Eastern Canada. Newell feels deeply that global energy needs can be met in Canada, through its massive reserves in the oilsands. Technology will continue to bring about secure and responsible energy growth.

"When we have all this development in this area, people worry about the cumulative effects. Yet we have quite a sophisticated process here and [federal environment minister] David Anderson uses it as his model. We have to look at the impact. Are we going so fast that we are creating an environmental problem we can't get out of? We are looking at overall limits of airshed and watershed quality and making sure that all the projects can be managed within," Newell says.

The Great Canadian Oil Sands, which was the first of the many oilsands projects in Fort McMurray, began production in 1967, and today is part of Suncor Energy. Rick George considers his company the pioneer in the area.

"We persevered through 25 really tough years before we found a lot of the keys. We made all the changes in the early '90s and this company went through all that, and then came the prosperity. Now people are trying to find out the way to get into the oilsands business and want to know what's the secret. Well, it was a lot of hard work by a lot people that preceded me," says George with a laugh. "It's a long-term relationship."[18]

Like Newell, George wants to reduce emissions. He shies away from any debate on the science of global climate change and focuses on the goal of fewer emissions from Suncor operations. Five years ago, Suncor invested $300 million for that purpose. As George points out, this was not a "must-do" project 20 years ago.

Over the last decade, Suncor has cut its CO_2 intensity by 16 per cent on a unit-of-production basis, and its SO_2 by 30 per cent. However, since Suncor's overall production has risen sharply over the same period, its emissions volumes have gone up, but at a much slower rate.

"We're heading in the right direction. If you look at that technology today, it does a lot to clean up the emissions. It is not a labour-intensive kind of thing—capital-intensive, yes," notes George.

"Remember, our industry is one that is built on large capital bets. You can think of that in terms of the oilsands, but it's also true in terms of refiners and pipelines. We are making decisions today that take us five years to implement—a couple of years to get regulatory approval and then three years of construction. So you're making bets that are out there five years."

That's why using the most innovative and current technology is crucial. It can cut costs, reduce emissions, and boost energy efficiency. "This is not an industry that turns on a dime. On the other hand, this is a huge technical industry, and a lot of the decisions we make are keyed off the same things that you'd expect, like efficiency and reducing emissions," adds George.

George also supports investing in alternative renewable energy. Suncor cast its net widely and examined a range of fuel sources such as methane from landfills, solar cells, and wind power. "The one thing that looks to be the most viable currently to us is wind power. I'm not saying those other technologies won't come. Many of those don't currently have an adequate rate of return, or a return even above our costs of capital. I've met with a number of the groups, and they'll say, 'Listen, you should invest in solar power.' I've looked at it. Can you find me a project with solar power in Canada that has a return above our costs of capital?" asks George.

Gordon Lambert, Suncor vice-president for sustainable development, feels technological advancement is the constant element of the oilpatch. Given the competition within the industry and the forces of the market outside, every producer searches constantly for more effective technology and more efficient operations. Lambert also sees trends like cogeneration, in which costs come down and the environmental benefits go up. Suncor built a large-scale cogeneration plant with TransAlta, and half the power that is generated goes onto the power grid, to be sold far away from the Fort McMurray plant.

"We've had more progress on the technical front. At our oil-sands sites, we used a technology called FGD—flue-gas desulphurization. We actually scrub sulphur emissions out of our combustion gases. This did transform the environmental performance of the oilsands operation on the order of a 90 per cent reduction of SO_2 emissions. It was dramatic," says Lambert.[19]

"Environmental control technology has been required of facilities being built here for many years. There was much foresight in putting in place emission control requirements and sulphur-recovery requirements by the regulators and it goes back many years. Some of the requirements being imposed on these facilities were well in advance of other jurisdictions doing that. We've adopted the preventive approach to undesirable environmental impacts, whereas virtually every other jurisdiction in the world is remedial and the damages of emissions are being addressed after the fact."

Dr. Brian Bietz is excited about future technological advances as well as companies combining their forces in such areas as road building and mapping, all to protect the environment. "We're probably going to see over the next two to three years a truly significant drop in the amount of emissions, particularly from the smaller facilities."[20]

He also forecasts the building of fewer gas plants. Instead, there will be more efficient standing operations and virtual gas processing. Producers will put raw gas into the pipeline and will then electronically take out processed gas. The actual ownership of the gas plant won't be significant as long as the producer gets the exact electronic amount to match what he or she put in as raw product. In the past, the producers wanted to control their own processing. What's important today is to optimize the return on capital investment. The gas will go to where it's most efficient, and it won't matter where it came from. Virtual processing means fewer but more efficient processing plants and a cleaner environment.

Energy efficiency and environmental respect go hand in hand. Whether the company is pumping oil or laying pipeline, the responsible one wants to minimize the costs to the land as well as to its balance sheets. Brian MacNeill, former CEO of pipeline giant Enbridge, explains that newer technologies can help companies determine how long the land that they've drilled will be scarred— right to the number of days. This allows for more efficient reclamation so the site is returned to its natural state much faster.

"Rightly or wrongly, the petroleum industry has a bad rap. There's seismic trucks and explosions and roads and rigs—it's all visual. With communications, it's instant—and you can't see it. You have to manage the issues more and have to be more conscious of your constituents," says MacNeill. "Pipelining is a little different. We have thousands and thousands of owners we have to deal with. The pipe is there forever and it's an ongoing issue."[21]

The regulations have become more stringent. Scraper pigs—cylindrical mechanical tools that squeal like a pig as they travel through the pipeline—inspect and clean the inside of the pipe. In the past, the waste would simply be dumped on the land and covered with sand, and that was it. No more. Now "smart pigs" work in a happier habitat. The technology is so sophisticated that the crack-detection devices are able to spot corrosion, cracking, and buckling inside the pipe.

"We run pigs quite frequently," says MacNeill. "We had a huge program for prevention and maintenance issues, so we put a sleeve on the pipe and had a program to strengthen the pipe. If we had to do hydro testing, we developed water farms, and by the time we processed it, the water was clean enough to drink. We also developed land farming, where we take contaminated land, put microbes in it, expose it to air, and reclaim it."

MacNeill is also a booster of northern resource operations where Aboriginals will once again become empowered through economic investment and other opportunities. Enbridge operated the Northern Wells pipeline for nearly 20 years, the only pipeline in the world functioning in permafrost.

"We developed the technology—chilling the oil before going in—and the work to prevent slippage. The technology is there to do the northern pipelines. The Alaska pipeline was going to destroy the caribou. The offshore industry was going to kill the shrimp. Instead they proliferated because they were protected. In the future the development has to be done in the right manner, through cooperation," he says.

Despite the highly competitive nature of oil and gas exploration, where industry scouts eagerly keep a shrewd eye on the competition, there's another linchpin that holds oilmen and oilwomen together—cooperation. Acclaimed author Fred Stenson, in his definitive history of gas processing in Canada called *Waste to Wealth*, discussed the cooperative nature of the industry as a whole.

"Since at least the 1950's, operators and supervisors in this country have been *leaning over the back fence* [sic], letting one another in on better ways of slowing down corrosion or better plans for stopping the foaming problems in an amine tower," writes Stenson.

"The willingness to co-operate and communicate is another fact that will probably ring untrue to some looking in on the industry from outside. The vision of dog-eat-dog capitalists, greedily hoarding their secrets, is a strong one in public folklore. Within the industry, the folklore of 'let's get the damn job done' is considerably stronger."[22]

By sharing best practices, industry has been able to boost its safety record and combine techniques for improving environmental performance. Part of that mentality is uniquely Canadian, which, as Stenson argued, reflected "a grass-roots tendency in the Canadian gas patch."

That grassroots stamp could be worn by any number of current Canadian leaders within the entire oilpatch. They've drilled down through accepted wisdom to challenge theories of the day as they search—some of them passionately—for better environmental answers and technologies.

Gwyn Morgan grew up working on his dad's farm in rural Alberta and spends a good part of his spare time in the country or in the mountains. The air was fresh when he was a kid tending the fields, and it still is. He feels the industry is good to the people and the environment in the rural areas.

"The fact is that the environment of these rural people compared to those living in the city would be a hundred times cleaner on any day you measure, in any city, even on a pretty good day. It's just the way it is. There's no concentration, unless people are living next to a pig farm or something like that.

"On the upstream [production] side of the business, we've gotten our stack stuff [facility emissions] pretty darn clean. Our stack heights are higher and the impact on people lower. What is still an issue, of course, is if you have a process upset and you have to flare. I think every operator is trying to have less of that and striving to become more reliable in their operations. We've gotten to be a pretty darn safe environment in the industry."

It's a long way from the days when waste gas was burned in huge flare pits. The one near Turner Valley, Alberta, was known as "hell's half-acre" and lit up the horizon for hundreds of miles, reverberating around the world, or at least as far as New York City.

A *New York World* editorial, which was reprinted in the *Calgary Herald* on June 23, 1925, described the scene and its consequences:

"Inhabitants of the Turner Valley oilfield up in Alberta, seem to be rather proud of the fact that the huge flaming jets of natural gas from one of their wells, burning day and night, have so warmed the land in the neighborhood that many wild flowers have bloomed weeks and weeks ahead of the right seasonal time. Instead, they ought to be ashamed to confess the waste of a precious commodity, and one that is even more precious in that region than in others where cheap fuel is less needed. They are only doing, however, what has been done again and again here in the United States—and now is bitterly regretted wherever the supply of natural gas is exhausted or failing fast."[23]

People used the natural gas to heat and light their homes, even though the smell of sour gas permeated the area. The putrid odour of naphtha, the liquid condensate from natural gas production, did nothing to deter the car and truck owners from using this "skunk oil" for gasoline. Skunk oil or not, the price was right. According to author Frank Dabbs, when naphtha was being produced, it was pretty sour, so people would cover their eyes with onion slices, which would turn black. The flowers may have bloomed earlier, but by July all the bushes in the area looked like they'd just remembered September.[24]

The federal government continued to control Alberta and Saskatchewan's natural resources until 1930, when Ottawa passed the Natural Resources Transfer Act. Producers were ultimately taken to task for the massive flaring of gas. In 1938 Alberta set up the Petroleum and Natural Gas Conservation Board, which quickly established procedures for flaring.

"We've come a huge distance," says Gwyn Morgan. "Even miscellaneous flaring is down substantially. The flaring issue is a bit of a red herring and a bit of a flashpoint."

Morgan notes that people don't realize that when some gas is being flared or when a plant is using natural gas to generate power, it's the same process as when home furnaces or hot water heaters start up.

"Take that power plant for a minute. It burns pure natural gas and has less impact on those homeowners that live in the area than their own pilot lights do," he says.

Morgan feels there's a major lack of scientific understanding on the part of those who cover the industry. Certainly there's an often sophisticated appreciation for the business aspect of production, but the actual science of petroleum exploration and production is woefully lost on many an otherwise good journalist.

"So they don't have any basis on which to realize when they're being fed crap and when they're not. If someone says this natural gas plant is going to have all these particulates and everything else, I'm wondering what is this person talking about. . . . The scary thing is that people believe it, and there isn't any sort of a common sense analogy made. People who are reporting on that plant can also say, 'Just a minute here, if you're burning natural gas from that plant, the citizens of Calgary burn about 50 times as much on a cool day doing exactly the same thing. But it doesn't burn quite as cleanly as that plant is going to burn, because your home furnaces aren't quite as efficient. The last thing we worry about is natural gas from furnaces, and quite properly so. It is absolutely one of the least things to worry about, because it is safe.

"So, if you're sitting beside a power plant, or sitting beside a gas flare—as long as it's not a sour gas flare—it's no different than what's in your furnace."

Morgan notes that the higher CO_2 levels actually foster more and faster plant growth. The boreal forest is growing, not shrinking, while the rainforest replenishes itself quickly (which doesn't mean that we should fail to protect it). More abundant plant life in turn means that more carbon is "fixed" in plants and taken out of the atmosphere.

He believes that the whole debate over global warming has actually turned attention away from improving the environment. "What we need to do when we talk about the environment is to concentrate on actual pollutants, not what you get when you burn natural gas, which is carbon dioxide and water," insists Morgan. "The issues where this industry needs to focus have gone from what happens with emissions associated with the upstream business, to the emissions that are associated with the consumption of the product."

That's why, over time, there's been a huge change in the tailpipe emissions of automobiles. There's no doubt that in a city, the vast majority of pollution comes from the cars.

"Down in Mexico City, in one of their usual traffic jams, I finally got out of the car and jogged back to the hotel," adds Morgan. "Everybody else got there an hour and a half later. But 10 years ago in that same traffic jam, I couldn't run, because I couldn't breathe. And there are more cars in Mexico now, but they are newer and the tailpipe emissions are probably a fiftieth of what they were only 10 years ago."

While cars are more environmentally friendly, SUVs still are not. Yet consumers demand and buy them in droves. Certainly the auto manufacturers have an obligation to convert them from truck to sedan standards. But it's ultimately the public that votes with its feet, and today too many of them remain on the gas pedals of their SUVs. The industry is trying to do its part as it develops and markets reformulated gasolines with less sulphur.

Petro-Canada vice-president Greta Raymond has seen the changes throughout her career in the industry and finds companies much more aware of their environmental impact. A more informed public now keeps companies talking and thinking green. It's a decided change from the past, when many companies smelled only one thing—money. Even the rotten-egg smell from small sour gas emissions was actually called just that—the smell of money.

"The proactive approach to the environment wasn't there. 'How can we not have oil spills?' wasn't asked," remembers Raymond. "Now it is much more proactive. There's structure around standards, policies, management systems, and emergency response systems. There's much more openness and transparency with external reporting. We talk about our record and our emissions so people can compare our company against another."[25]

Auditing environmental performance and releasing the findings wasn't done 20 years ago. Neither was working with environmental groups like the Pembina Institute to change a company's vision and practice.

Pembina had been hired by Petro-Canada for a workshop concerning its oilsands project. Raymond's group agreed to try Pembina's Life Cycle Value Assessment, but the oilsands engineers were skeptical. They felt the exercise would not only be a waste of time, but would also keep them from their important engineering work. During an intense brainstorming session, they were asked to design a technology that they could use to reduce the company's environmental impact.

The engineers agreed to try it. They become very creative and developed ideas for reducing emissions while also saving the company money. When the engineers were considering a pipeline replacement project in Montreal, they were able to quantify the human impact of digging up the streets in front of people's homes.

"These exercises were engineer-focused. Pembina's Life Cycle Value Assessment has opened people's eyes," says Raymond. "All companies have their own personal experiences where they realize that trying to fight anything or trying to do it the cheapest way ends up costing money. So they end up getting religion."

That religion is environmental sustainability. The Pembina Institute has been in business since 1985 and uses policy forums, regulatory interventions, direct negotiations, independent papers, and the media to educate business, the public, and government about the environmental impact of energy consumption and production. Pembina's Tom Marr-Laing is pleased that the industry has cut its flaring rate by 53 per cent. Now he'd like to see energy companies reduce their footprint on the land itself.

"There's still some work to be done in coalescing public opinion around land-base problems," says Marr-Laing. "The air issues—particularly flaring—had some actual elements that made it much more attractive in forming public opinion. [People could see the flares burning.] On the basis of eco-efficiency, producers have been improving and progressive companies are good."[26]

That said, Marr-Laing believes economics are more likely to drive environmentally just decisions, rather than a pure corporate conscience. For the most part, he's right. The industry certainly didn't lead in environmental initiatives, and in many cases lagged behind. That's now changing, thanks to public pressure and the push from people working within the industry.

While Marr-Laing has worked effectively from outside to change the petroleum industry's environmental conscience, people like Barry Worbets have toiled tenaciously from within. Worbets has seen the relationship between the petroleum and forestry industries improve dramatically over the years.

"The common issue throughout my career is how we've used the land and water," says Barry Worbets, who has spent over 25 years in the oilpatch.[27]

Worbets worked in the Beaufort Sea and did his master's degree in oil spills and planning, the big issue of the 1970s. During the next decade the focus was sour gas and acid rain. The first impor-tant discussions on climate change began in the 1990s. Worbets remembers the changes in the industry since the 1970s, when seismic activity took more logs from the Alberta landscape than the logging industry did.

"The seismic business has done a total 180-degree on land-use practices. They've moved from a huge impact to zero impact, and they can do it in a far more economic and efficient way than ever," says Worbets.

The security and safety of the water supply has always been a crucial issue for the petroleum industry. The public wants to know, and has a right to know, if the refinery close by or the well or the sour gas plant or the service station has any impact on the quality and quantity of the drinking water.

Another major issue is the environmental liability of facilities that have been in operation for many years, are coming to a close, and need to be cleaned up in accordance with stricter guidelines than when they were initially built. The industry's orphan well program takes care of the negligent who ditched their responsibil-ities, but the responsible companies know they must clean the area and reclaim it.

"We have to do things a lot better in the wilderness areas," says Worbets. "There are still those who operate with a frontier mental-ity. The Alberta government, along with the petroleum and forest industries, is working well to create financial wealth, but we need to take a long-term view to protect and sustain our incredible nat-ural wealth. I'm a practical environmentalist and see so much room for improvements in our practices. But we're lemming-like."

When Worbets leads his workshop "Conservation Biology and Implications for Policy," he begins with these words: "Access to land is our industry's most important public policy issue. We must operate properly or we are out of business." Then he presents his principles for development:

- Engage in early and meaningful consultation.
- Co-exist with present and future uses and users.
- Coordinate industry activities to minimize disturbance and duplication of infrastructure and activity.
- Undertake appropriate environmental assessment and protection.
- Minimize footprint.
- Reduce or avoid environmental impact through consultation, planning, design, innovation, and technology.

Placing innovation above convention is the growing practice of industry leaders tackling ecological challenges in sensitive areas. They use global positioning systems to assess and map areas that wildlife use as migration corridors or as a habitat. Wildlife safety can be monitored through laser or infrared techniques, while DNA assessment can measure whether birds and animals have been pushed from their homes or tempted to remain.

Minimizing the footprint has become an industry mantra. In ecologically sensitive areas, it exudes urgency. When Worbets worked on Husky Energy's controversial Moose Mountain project, he wanted minimal intrusions during the whole development. That meant 3 drilling pads with a potential for 16 directional wells, rather than overwhelming the popular hiking and camping area with 16 separate drilling pads. Over 90 per cent of the development took full advantage of existing disturbances, while pipelines and roads were constructed within the same corridor. Worbets made a point of constant communication with forestry and recreational groups.

Responsible producers don't wait for regulators and landowners to tell them how to leave the land footprint-free. They use heli-seismic, directional drilling, and multi-well pads. They're eliminating flares and reducing venting, while also building berms to cut noise and hide any unsightly equipment.

"Being a good neighbour goes a long way," says Worbets. "Now we work to hide the well and its site. In one area, the well site is shaped like a natural meadow—it's not an ugly square cement box in the middle of a pristine landscape. The technological changes and innovations are astounding. You can run a well site from a PC in your home that is tied to a satellite."

Investment banker Michael Tims, the CEO of Peters & Co., has covered energy companies for 25 years. He likes the industry's growing focus on environmental sustainability and corporate responsibility. As a banker, he readily identifies with the associated financial costs of a corporate conscience, but feels they are an integral part of doing business.

"Some of the companies are much more out in front of the issues than they ever would have been 25 years ago," he says. "That's due in part to the higher sensitivity among the public. But all the strong companies will want to be seen at best-practices level. In general, they want to be on the good side. It benefits them in the market and in public."[28]

At every stage within the industry, environmental challenges exist. During exploration, companies cut seismic lines and shuttle drilling machinery to the site. There's the full preparation of the site, and then the drilling. Pipelines are built to deliver the oil or gas from the wells to the gathering systems. More pipelines carry the petroleum to the refinery.

Every phase features its own environmental challenges and solutions. At the seismic stage, an alternative to the all-encompassing Caterpillar cut is a hand-cut or heli-portable seismic. Global positioning systems are a terrific advance for siting shot holes and doing seismic exploration because operators can be very precise and cut under the canopy. During intense exploration in sensitive areas, companies can use closed-system testing, where few emissions escape into the environment.

The portable compressors can be taken from one site to another. Twenty years ago, they stayed put. Modern refineries meet today's stringent environmental guidelines and have replaced most of the old, inefficient plants.

"There's still room for improvement, but we're vast steps ahead of where we were 20 years ago. Operating practices are much better now," notes Tims. "We have a cottage at Sylvan Lake [in central Alberta] and an oil and gas company was drilling a well about a hundred yards off our property line. Someone asked if we complained and I said no. I know they manage the testing and gave notices and were the least invasive in their operating practices. They're sensitive to the environment and realize if they do it right they'll have far less complaints. They did a terrific job drilling in cottage country."

Bill Clapperton's role is to make sure those jobs are done right. As vice-president of regulatory, stakeholder, and environmental affairs for Canadian Natural Resources, he tours the countryside where his company has operations, making sure that the environment and the people on the land are respected. "The biggest thing we're doing differently is fitting into the footprint," he says. "There are smaller disturbances, less emissions per barrel of production, greater energy efficiency, and a lot of containment."[29]

Martha Kostuch wants a whole lot more. For the last 20 years, she's clamoured for much of the change now seen in the oilpatch, and she has no intention of stopping. "Are there still problems?" she asks. "Yes. One is chronic from ongoing exposure to sulphur dioxide in stacks. It affects the animals' reproductive systems, causing spontaneous abortions and stillbirths, as well as a lower immune system. The second are acute problems associated with flaring, blowouts, and pipeline leaks."[30]

Even though a ground-breaking study is underway to examine those issues, Kostuch isn't waiting. She intends to carry on using whatever method it takes—and always non-violent—to bring the companies to her level of understanding.

"Flaring has been reduced by 50 per cent, which is quite an accomplishment. People and farmers working around those flares have noticed quite an improvement. The goal is to eliminate flares and we're working on venting and further reductions."

Kostuch is pleased that two of her projects, reducing SO_2 emissions from the Ram River and Strachan plants in Alberta, have been successful. Today their SO_2 emissions are 20 per cent of what they were in 1982.

Today also, the best companies in the oilpatch publish environmental audits of their accomplishments and failures. It's quite the thing to see a company of the stature of Shell Canada declare its mistakes in its own very public report *Progress Toward Sustainable Development*. Shell is upfront when it discusses the $150,000 fine it paid for discharging fumes into the environment in 1998, and the $2,500 for excess SO_2 emissions in 1999. Its CEO, Tim Faithfull, wrote about the rocky journey toward sustainability.

"Like many worthwhile journeys, the path is neither smooth nor simple. In some areas we surged ahead, as this year when we were able to declare that all halon, an ozone-depleting substance, was removed from our operations; and when we announced record earnings. In other areas we were very disappointed, as when a combination of factors led to an unignited flare release at our Sarnia facility, which impacted the local community; and when our contractor safety performance, though improving, failed to meet our target."[31]

Shell also presents its successes, including reducing CO_2 emissions and stabilizing greenhouse-gas emissions to 1990 levels. The company plans to be 6 per cent below its 1990 levels by 2008 (thus beating Canada's proposed Kyoto target). Faithfull declares that in being transparent and honest, Shell's sustainability goals and assumptions can be examined by others like the Pembina Institute. In its report, Shell included this message from Pembina's Climate Change Program director, Robert Hornung.

"The Pembina Institute believes Shell Canada must ensure that business expansion does not increase corporate greenhouse-gas emissions. We are hopeful that the Advisory Panel will help Shell Canada identify and implement innovative mechanisms to meet this objective," states Hornung.[32]

Suncor's *Report on Sustainability* has CEO Rick George discussing a journey similar to that of Tim Faithfull and bluntly discussing areas "where we need to improve." Ron Brenneman, the CEO of Petro-Canada, offers similar assessments in the company's *Report to the Community* and notes that economic performance isn't the only indicator of a company's contribution to society.

"Rather, the extent of our company's operational influence, and ultimate impact—both positive and negative—must be evaluated in light of our environmental and societal contributions, as well as our financial performance," says Brenneman.[33]

Nexen CEO Charlie Fischer works closely with vice-president Randall Gossen on Nexen's annual report on safety, environment, and social responsibility. Like the others, they report their environmental incidents and successes, and apply their standards globally.

"Of note is the fact that our contractors and landowners are now actively assisting us in identifying potential problems so that they can be addressed proactively," they write. "For 2002, Nexen Canada will establish additional performance criteria which will better reflect the frequency and significance of environmental incidents, including number of spills per unit of production."[34]

These are the best companies, and yet they're not afraid to admit their mistakes as they strive to better their environmental performance. Gwyn Morgan included this responsibility as an integral part of the constitution of Alberta Energy, which he headed before it merged with PanCanadian Energy to become EnCana. By making community and environmental responsibility official policy, Morgan was telling employees and the public that this was a fundamental value not to be tampered with: "Together, we share in the responsibility of working safely and caring for the environment," the constitution stated.[35]

Morgan brought that commitment to EnCana. As he considered a name for the large new company, its logo, and colours—which became blue and green—he went back to the history and values of

AEC and PanCanadian: "The blue represents water and sky. The green represents Earth, suggesting growth and reinforcing our commitment to the environment."[36]

This approach has become the norm within Canada's best energy companies as they strive to become green, and their recalcitrant siblings are forced to follow by the regulators and public opinion.

CHAPTER SEVEN

The Accord

M any Canadians have always felt ambivalent, resentful, and even guilty about our domestic oil and gas business. We are among the most profligate energy users in the world, yet hostility to the industry that produces much of that energy is common, especially in provinces that provide little or none. In the 1970s and 1980s, when the OPEC cartel held sway over prices and supply, we had a national crisis over oil and gas that caused Ottawa to launch the National Energy Program. The NEP of 1980 had two key policy goals: to help Canada become self-sufficient, and to exploit oil and gas on federal lands, thus reducing provincial control. This reflected an enduring tension among governing Liberal politicians: They realize that the constitution guarantees that oil and gas found within provincial boundaries belongs to the provinces, but still feel that petroleum is essentially a strategic national resource. By attempting to control both the price of oil and the very places where the industry would operate, the federal government was attacking a fundamental national agreement. The producing provinces, especially Alberta, reacted fiercely to what was widely seen as a cash and power grab that the government never would have tried in Ontario or Quebec.[1]

The provincial side scored a major victory in 1986 when the Conservative government of Prime Minister Brian Mulroney abolished the NEP and later brought in free trade, which allowed less restricted sale of oil and gas to the United States. By that time the NEP was irrelevant anyway, because the ever-rising prices it postulated faded away in the face of reduced OPEC control and ample supplies. In a world flush with energy, the idea of self-sufficiency gradually faded from the national agenda, although the industry continued to promote it.

Now the national mood is even more peculiar, as reflected in the divisive debate on ratification of the 1997 Kyoto Protocol, which would require sharp reductions in the national production of greenhouse gases, especially carbon dioxide. Before it can take effect there must be 55 ratifying countries representing 55 percent of the emissions addressed by the Protocol. By late 2002 more than 55 countries had ratified, but their total emissions came to only 36.6 per cent.

On September 2 Prime Minister Jean Chrétien announced in South Africa that Canada would ratify by the end of the year. This adds only 3 per cent to the emissions total, bringing the percentage to 39—still far short of the amount needed for worldwide implementation of the treaty. But Chrétien, as expected, touched off a furious national debate that threatened to set provinces and citizens against each other. Those who appropriate the environmental agenda accuse the naysayers of self-interest, while Kyoto opponents argue that the Accord will cripple the economy without solving global warming, if that phenomenon even exists in the form promoted by pro-Kyoto scientists.

Many experts argue that human-made emissions are warming the planet, while others, equally distinguished, deny this or say the case is not proven. Some of this gas is sent into the atmosphere when oil and gas are produced, but the vast majority comes from the consumption of fossil fuels by cars, trucks, home heating, and industry. Canada cannot possibly meet Kyoto obligations without sharply cutting emissions in all these areas. Yet there's a prevailing national impression, not often discouraged by federal government politicians, that the producing industry will somehow bear the main burden. Greenpeace, the militant environmental group, is more even-handed. One of its provocative studies says that tougher vehicle-emission standards could meet one-third of Canada's Kyoto commitments.[2]

To the extent that Ottawa wants to curb consumption, it flirts with punitive taxation measures such as toll roads, higher parking fees, and levies on fuel-guzzling sport utility vehicles. Some of the money would then be used to buy foreign emission credits—a tactic that doesn't seem to please anyone. Kyoto opponents say this is simply disguised foreign aid, while the environmental groups argue that buying credits avoids action on pollution at home.

A federal government Web site for Agriculture and Agri-Food Canada shows the burden of the Kyoto obligations and how widely they must be spread if Canada is to have any chance of complying after signing the treaty.[3] "In the Kyoto protocol," it says, "Canada agreed to reduce its emissions to 94 per cent of 1990 levels by 2008 to 2012. But Canada's emissions are already well above 1990 levels. Based on increases from 1990 to 1997 and assuming a 'business as usual' scenario thereafter, one estimate suggests that Canada will need to reduce its emissions by about 21 per cent. Consequently, a widespread effort involving all sectors of our economy will be required to meet Canada's commitments." The 21 per cent estimate is probably optimistic; current calculations of Canada's obligation run closer to 26 per cent, and it could be even higher if the economy is strong. The debate over the Protocol has brought apocalyptic predictions from both sides. *National Post* columnist Diane Francis says that to reduce emissions by 6 per cent from 1990 levels, we would have to stop all economic growth until 2010—and even this wouldn't quite reach the requirement to cut 139 megatonnes. Other measures that would meet part of the Kyoto target include converting all thermal power plants to nuclear energy; taking half of Canada's vehicles off the road; tripling gasoline prices; imposing a total ban on exports from forestry, oil and gas, mining, chemicals, and cement. The last measure would eliminate one-third of all the private-sector jobs in Canada, Francis says. Outlawing cars forever would save only 45 megatonnes of emissions, less than one-third of Canada's obligation.[4]

The David Suzuki Foundation, on the other hand, predicts ecological calamity if Kyoto isn't signed, and then presents it as a boon, not just to the environment, but to the economy as well. A report released by the foundation in June 2002 says: "Recent modelling work by the U.S.-based Tellus Institute demonstrates that implementing energy efficiency measures and other Kyoto-compliant policies in Canada produces positive economic benefits. An additional 52,000 jobs would be created through domestic action on the Kyoto target. Unlike large fossil-fuel projects, these jobs are created in all areas of the country, ensuring that all regions benefit from the move to a more energy efficient economy. As well, Canada's GDP would increase by $2 billion and average household income would grow by $135 beyond business as usual projections."[5]

The foundation also says that with carbon dioxide valued at $10 per tonne, emissions reduction measures for economic sectors, and a trading system for large fossil-fuel users, the economy would actually grow 30.4 per cent by 2012, including a 24.6 per cent increase in the oil and gas sector. (This is an odd prediction, considering that the whole thrust of foundation policy is to slash consumption of fossil fuels.) Suzuki's group opposes any further concessions to provide credits for our clean-energy exports, on the grounds that they encourage energy use in both Canada and the United States.[6]

Whatever the truth of these wildly varying predictions, there is no doubt that Canada agreed to the most onerous conditions of any major oil-and-gas–producing nation. Another federal govern-

ment summary outlines the details: "At Kyoto, developed countries agreed to reduce their combined emissions of greenhouse
gases by 5.2 per cent from 1990 levels. This target will be realized
through national reductions of eight per cent by Switzerland,
many Central and East European states, and the European Union;
reductions of seven per cent by the United States; and reductions
of six per cent by Canada, Hungary, Japan, and Poland. Russia,
New Zealand, and Ukraine are to stabilize their emissions, while
Norway may increase emissions by one per cent, Australia by up to
eight per cent, and Iceland by 10 per cent."[7]

This reveals the inequality of the Protocol. Many European
countries have experienced low growth for a decade and don't
produce oil and gas. Germany has improved its record by closing
inefficient plants in the former East Germany, something that had
to be done in any case. These and similar advantages in other
countries make the European targets relatively easy to meet. Yet
Norway, a producing country, managed to negotiate an increase in
emissions. Iceland gets a 10 per cent increase to account for
growth and Australia 8 per cent, while Russia only needs to "stabilize"—a relatively easy target because oil consumption in Russia
has shrunk drastically due to economic stagnation. Yet Russia still
had not ratified as this was being written in early September 2002.

Australia, meanwhile, rejected the treaty outright despite its
advantageous deal. "For us to ratify the Protocol would cost us jobs
and damage our industry," Prime Minister John Howard told the
Australian Parliament on June 5, 2002.[8] He added that Australia
would not reconsider unless the United States and other developed nations agree to Kyoto—an unlikely prospect for many years
to come. The OPEC nations are not part of the Protocol at all and
the Americans have rejected it flatly. Canada, alone among large
energy producers and exporters, agreed to sharp reductions.[9]

Allan MacRae, an engineer and investment banker who has
worked in Europe and the former Soviet Union, caught the

contradictions in a *National Post* column in which he noted that Canada has had more population growth than Europe and hence a stronger economy, partly through immigration. "Because we have had greater economic growth than Europe since 1990, we will need to buy even more CO_2 credits than if we had a slower economy. Should the Europeans be rewarded and Canada pay huge fines for credits, just because we have a better economy and welcomed more immigrants?"[10]

Technically, other countries in the western hemisphere have signed and ratified the Protocol: They include Argentina, Bolivia, Cuba, the Dominican Republic, Ecuador, El Salvador, Guatemala, Honduras, Paraguay, Peru, Trinidad and Tobago, Uruguay, and— most important for Canada—Mexico. But none of these nations is subject to emission quotas. They are not obliged to do anything to meet the Kyoto targets, although they can benefit from efforts by the developed signatories to meet their own (more on this later). Essentially, these countries can sign Kyoto without environmental obligation because it was agreed that their priorities are development and the reduction of poverty, while developed nations have an obligation to help them curb greenhouse gases.

Ralph Klein, Alberta's premier, compares Kyoto to the NEP in its impact on the economies of his province and several others that produce oil and gas. Academics have long claimed that the NEP cost the province at least $60 billion in lost revenues and investment, in 1980s dollars. Alberta feels Kyoto could be even more devastating, with dire results not just for provincial revenues, but for Ottawa's as well. In 2001, the national petroleum industry paid $14 billion to governments in royalties, bonuses, fees, and income tax. In British Columbia, oil and gas provided $1.8 billion to the province, more than forestry, for the first time ever. Alberta is now one of only two "have" provinces in the country, contributing with Ontario to all the others through the equalization formula. With Kyoto in force, it's probable that only Ontario would remain in the black—and maybe not for long, considering that the largest province could no longer compete on equal footing with powerful neighbours such as New York and Michigan.

Former Alberta premier Peter Lougheed, who fought the original NEP battle, is appalled at the dangers. "The stakes are enormous and the implications are as great as the NEP," he says. "But it was much easier to fight the NEP than Kyoto."[11] In September he cautioned that Alberta should have a "Plan B" ready to implement "if Ottawa is foolish enough to ratify." Lougheed's own measures during the NEP fight of 1980–81 included cutting oil shipments to the rest of Canada and challenging a federal export tax in the Supreme Court.[12]

Much of the offhand rejection of Alberta's views seems to be based on the idea that the province is wildly prosperous and can afford to contribute. But Alberta already does. A draft study by DRI-WEFA, an international think tank, shows that although Alberta produces more per capita wealth than any other province ($49,000 compared to $37,100 for Ontario), much of it is already redistributed around the country through equalization payments and corporate taxes. While per capita wealth is 40 per cent higher than the average in Canada, disposable income is only 10 per cent higher than average.[13] This is clear evidence that Alberta's oil wealth benefits the entire country, and that any shrinkage in the province's economy will hurt everyone.

Nonetheless, Alberta at first found itself virtually alone as it raised the alarm about Kyoto. The government threatened to use tactics similar to the tough actions of the 1980s. Klein and his environment minister, Lorne Taylor, consistently implied that the province would refuse to write legislation to enable the Kyoto Protocol. Taylor also raised the spectre of the province taking the issue to the Supreme Court. "I'm not sure we'll have to go forward to a Supreme Court challenge," Taylor said at one point. "I hope not. I hope we will be able to negotiate with the federal government as they . . . develop a plan that is both acceptable to Alberta and the federal government."[14] That hope seemed to be gone by early September, when Taylor again said Alberta was preparing a court challenge along with the province's own plan to meet emission targets by 2020.

Alberta and any other provinces that choose to oppose Ottawa's measure will have plenty of ammunition. A federal plan for implementing the treaty is bound to interfere with provincial development of resources, as well as control over the environment. Ottawa argues that environment is a shared jurisdiction, but the provinces have long had their own environment departments with major responsibility. Alberta and any other province would obviously have a strong case in the courts, where there are powerful precedents for provincial victory. In the 1980s Alberta shocked Ottawa by winning a Supreme Court ruling against a federal export tax on natural gas. The court said Ottawa had overstepped the constitution by taxing another level of government.[15] The fundamental issue in any Kyoto challenge would be much the same: Is the federal government allowed to set aside constitutional guarantees when it writes laws, even to give force to international treaties?

Kyoto is a far more difficult and divisive issue than most others, including the National Energy Program. The NEP was a Canadian regional battle fought on an economic battlefield, while Kyoto is painted in almost religious terms as a struggle for the survival of the planet. It is hardly that. Even if the climate is warming because of human activity, Kyoto's impact on the problem would be minimal, considering that all the OPEC countries, representing the vast bulk of the world's oil production, as well as China, would be outside of the treaty. "Kyoto is very arbitrary," says Eric Newell, the CEO of Syncrude. "The largest emitters aren't signatories, so Kyoto won't help on the environmental side. Kyoto is one of the poorest-understood issues by Canadians."[16]

The argument of Kyoto boosters that other countries will sign on if we set an example seems naïve at best. Those countries are far more likely to exploit their new economic advantage to the hilt, but even that prospect doesn't trouble many of the Protocol's zealots. In a 1998 meeting with the editorial board of the *Calgary Herald*, Christine Stewart, the former federal environment minister, said that even if global warming isn't taking place, Kyoto is a good way to promote international economic equity.[17] The government seems willing to pay vast amounts to buy credits from other countries—money that would be raised in Canada and simply sent off without any productive benefit to the country.

Whether Canadians like it or not, the American rejection of Kyoto has a major impact on our decision. There's hardly a business leader in Canada who isn't uneasy about signing an international deal that will not bind our major trading partner, one that already enjoys huge advantages of scale and a powerful currency. The Canadian Council of Chief Executive Officers calls for a made-in-Canada program to cut emissions. Manufacturers and exporters predict the loss of 450,000 jobs. Rick George, Suncor's CEO, expressed the fears of many when he said, "For us to be the single ratifier of Kyoto . . . [puts us] in a very difficult position. I'm in favour of a made-in-Canada solution that makes sense for us as Canadian citizens, and for us as Canadian companies. To me, that doesn't mean following Europe or blindly following some international agreement."[18]

For the oil and gas industry, the economics of Kyoto are far more certain than the science. If the Protocol imposes emission standards that oil companies cannot meet economically, there could be a flight of capital from the industry. Stocks would be dumped and interests sold out. Much of the cash would end up in the hands of Americans who hold large stakes. The investors will then sit on that money until the companies lose so much value that it's attractive to buy them back. As financier Murray Edwards has pointed out, one major risk of Kyoto is virtually complete American ownership of the Canadian oilpatch.

A parallel possibility is the sharp erosion of investment capital in the industry. Lougheed predicts at the very least a "pause" in investment as outsiders, particularly Americans, try to figure how ratification will change the rules.[19]

The potential damage is especially acute in the oilsands, the largest oil reserve on the planet. Oilsands extraction is more costly than conventional operations and highly dependent on technology. The industry had struggled for 20 years to reduce the cost per barrel of producing this oil. Finally the sands are profitable and vast development is planned, but significant new costs could throw all this into doubt. Indeed, Kyoto would force the entire industry, which has been growing for years to meet demand, to shrink drastically. It's hard to imagine a greater reversal of the principles of the National Energy Program. The NEP at least considered the industry to be important, while Kyoto advocates seem to want it to disappear. The common thread, always present in Canada, is hostility.

From the very moment the Canadian government gave preliminary approval to Kyoto in 1997, the industry recognized the challenge and reacted by striving to reduce its emissions. Sensible leaders knew that in order to be credible in the coming debate, oil and gas companies had to improve. And they did, by cutting flaring by 53 per cent, by reducing leakage and venting of gas, and through a host of other measures. But the industry was growing at the same time because demand was high through much of the late 1990s and into the new century. Total emissions rose even as emissions per unit of production fell. More gains in reducing emissions can be made, but as one executive says, the "low-hanging fruit" has already been picked. Further improvements, although certainly desirable and essential, will be more difficult and costly. Logic leads to an inescapable conclusion: In order for the oil and gas industry to meet Kyoto targets, it would have to produce less.

Kyoto's system of credits is supposed to mitigate this problem for governments and industries, but Canada is already at a serious disadvantage because of Ottawa's inexplicable failure to negotiate credits for our clean-energy exports to the United States. Critics often point out that the Americans have a better emissions record than Canada does, but they seldom add that the United States looks good because they use our clean-burning natural gas. On the Kyoto balance sheet, Canada is stuck with the emissions released to produce that gas, but gets no recognition for the benefits to others.

For private companies the Kyoto challenge is huge, and the survival tactics they use could well be counterproductive to Kyoto's goals. Firms that need Kyoto credits because they operate high-emission facilities would be able to get them by helping solve a problem in another country, while doing nothing about their own emissions. Grant Patrick, an Alberta lawyer who works frequently in Latin America, paints the following scenario:

A Canadian company—an electricity generator that uses coal, for instance—needs credits to offset its relatively "dirty" domestic operation. If it converts a generator to natural gas in Alberta, the plant won't be able to compete in the province's deregulated marketplace; the price of electricity will simply be too high. So the company looks for a project in a less developed country in order to gain offsetting credits (under Kyoto, this is called a Clean Development Mechanism). It could find one in, for instance, Mexico, by helping a coal-fired plant convert to natural gas. The Canadian company would find this attractive because its bottom line would continue to show a profitable domestic plant. In essence, the company would help solve a pollution problem far away while ignoring one at home. Patrick says, "Although the concept of the CDM initially sounds great, their use will, in my opinion, simply disguise the true effect of the quota system while negatively impacting society by forcing businesses to import someone else's pollution problem and by deferring the correction of its own problems, all at an additional cost to the consumer."[20]

Kyoto could produce many other unpredictable results, even among countries that sign on as full participants. Japan ratified the Protocol on June 3, 2002—and immediately said it might meet its commitments by building nuclear power plants. Takeo Hiranuma, the minister of economy, trade and industry, told a press conference that nuclear energy policies are important in schemes to deal with global warming. "For instance, a 130-million-kilowatt nuclear-power plant helps cut carbon dioxide by 0.7 per cent. Theoretically, ten such plants could help reduce the gas by 7 per cent," Hiranuma said.[21] At the same time as Japan was signing, the Greenpeace Web site was running a horrifying feature from Russia called "Half Life—Living with the Effects of Nuclear Waste." Even moderate environmentalists shudder at the thought of nations building flocks of nuclear plants to win Kyoto points. Nothing in the Protocol stops this from happening.

In Canada, a string of industry and business organizations predicted disaster for the economy if Canada signed on while the United States did not. A federal–provincial meeting ended in acrimony when Alberta walked out, furious that its plan for meeting Kyoto targets at a later date wouldn't be part of the consultation process. Other provinces later said they supported parts of the plan, which essentially would meet Kyoto targets on a delayed timetable. By August 2002, the full annual premiers' meeting again rejected Alberta's stand, while cautiously refusing to endorse ratifying Kyoto. Kyoto had always been popular with most Canadians, but as time passed, the federal government's own polling began to reveal that as Canadians' knowledge of Kyoto grows, their support for it declines.[22] A growing chorus of scientists announced their objections to the certainties of Kyoto "science," especially the link between carbon dioxide and global warming. Their views began to be publicized in the media and widely distributed on the Internet. Early objections that had been ignored in the rush to Kyoto were dusted off by critics. One of the most telling was written in

1992 by Richard S. Lindzen, Sloan Professor of Meteorology at the Massachusetts Institute of Technology. "As a scientist, I can find no substantive basis for the warming scenarios being popularly described," he wrote. "Many aspects of the catastrophic scenario have already been largely discounted by the scientific community." He went on to dissect the science that was already paving the road to Kyoto, and concluded that the only unanimity was political, not scientific.[23] Dr. Lindzen was still making the same objections in 2001 as a member of a U.S. National Academy of Sciences panel on climate change (see Chapter Eight). Under all this pressure, the federal cabinet began to show cracks. In May 2002, industry minister Allan Rock sent a letter to cabinet colleagues urging them to consider a made-in-Canada plan as an alternative to Kyoto. "We should develop scenarios for a Canadian plan that takes action on climate change and considers our unique position in the North American context while leaving open the Kyoto target as a possible step along the way," the minister wrote in a memo obtained by the *Globe and Mail*. He added: "We must find ways to stay competitive while taking action on climate change. When the United States changed their position on ratifying Kyoto, it dramatically changed the playing field for Canada."[24] There wasn't much in his assessment for industry leaders to disagree with.

By June, energy minister Herb Dhaliwal seemed to be softening on Kyoto too, when he reiterated that Canada must be allowed credit for clean-energy exports to the United States. "The Americans are not signing on, we're a huge exporter into the U.S., and, overall, we reduce greenhouse-gas emissions as a result of exports of clean-energy funnels to the U.S.," he said. Since the Europeans seem obdurate on this issue, it's hard to see how Canada could sign without acknowledging that the economy will suffer severe damage.[25] Environment minister David Anderson still sounded devoted to Kyoto, but that was hardly surprising given his record and his portfolio. The cabinet's divisions were becoming unmistakable, and Premier Klein took heart. He said Alberta's constitutional challenge "is on the back burner now. The federal government appears to be moving towards not ratifying the Kyoto Protocol. Now we have breathing space. We're not interested in getting into a fight with Ottawa now. We want to resolve the issues together."

But then Chrétien, after his long leadership battle with Paul Martin, announced that he'll retire in 2004, and set about creating his "legacy." Earlier pledges to negotiate clean-export credits before ratifying seemed to vanish. He made his promise to ratify, and Alberta immediately cried betrayal. Lougheed caught the mood of many when he said, "Alberta is being penalized for its strength, 22 years later, at almost the same time of year. So we have to fight back the way we did in 1980–81."[26]

The public's main problem with Kyoto, perhaps, is the shortage of credible voices. The predictions of economic doom fostered by some industry groups are self-interested, while many environmentalists paint industry and anyone who opposes Kyoto as evil incarnate. The Suzuki Foundation accuses industry of scare tactics, but indulges in plenty of its own, with public relations zeal that would make a tobacco company blush. One of its Web site reports, called "Canada and the Kyoto Climate Treaty," starts with a doctored photo of the House of Commons, showing a desert landscape in the foreground and a Mountie riding a camel. The caption says: "How hot does it have to get before they ratify Kyoto?"

But one environmental group, the Pembina Institute for Appropriate Development, has earned a reputation for being practical, honest, and dedicated. Based in Alberta, with an active office in Ottawa, Pembina benefits from detailed knowledge of how the industry operates. It takes a pro-Kyoto stand, but also points to many domestic actions that governments and industry can take with or without the Protocol.

There's no doubting Pembina's attitude to Kyoto—it wants Canada to ratify the Protocol at the earliest possible moment. It says the cries of economic disaster don't take into account benefits from new technology and clear rules for investors. Pembina does acknowledge that there are "legitimate concerns about Canada's short-term competitiveness with respect to the United States if Canada ratifies . . . while the United States does not."[27] But these concerns are overstated, Pembina adds, because the U.S. withdrawal will lower the price of international credits, and cost increases to Canadian business will not be large in any case.

Industry would quarrel with some of that, but Pembina then goes on to offer a whole range of "domestic" options. In effect, Pembina outlines a program that could reduce Canadian greenhouse-gas emissions without ratifying Kyoto. The measures include domestic emissions credits, equity of financial costs among regions, and a transition period for high-emission geographic areas. Unlike industry, the Institute doesn't place much stock in voluntary measures. Pembina wants governments to enforce compliance: "Financial incentives for low emissions should be balanced by financial penalties for high emissions."[28] If Kyoto passes, the Institute wants Canada to buy as few international credits as possible to ensure that we do our own environmental work.

Everything in this system could function without Canada ever signing the Protocol—especially since we're so far behind the United States in some areas of emission control. Another Pembina study shows that many American states have adopted greenhouse-gas emission caps, often with support from federal programs, even as the White House rejects Kyoto on the political level.[29] No Canadian provinces have taken similar action (although the Eastern provinces, in cooperation with New England states, have set "goals" for emission reduction). Pembina says it's a fallacy to assume that because of the Bush administration's high-profile rejection of Kyoto, nothing is happening in the United States to reduce emissions. The study points to a great many measures, including California's Zero Emission Vehicles Program, New York's incentives for purchasing non-gasoline vehicles, and Minnesota's promotion of ethanol-blend gasoline. It argues convincingly that because of all this, Canada could do much without reducing competitiveness.[30] Once again, it must be said that Pembina supports Kyoto and doesn't intend its studies to be used as ammunition against the Protocol. But they nonetheless provide abundant evidence that action can be taken at all levels of government and industry, without subjecting Canada to the formal constraints of an international treaty.

The agenda of many environmentalists is propelled by a desire to force a massive switch to "clean" energy such as wind and solar power as soon as possible. The trouble is that these forms of energy cannot be produced in quantities sufficient to supply more than a fraction of world demand, and they won't for many years, no matter how ardently governments and companies pursue this objective. "Suzuki wants to see a world off oil, and maybe that will happen some day," says Gary Webster, formerly of the Canadian Association of Petroleum Producers. "But solar and wind power are still small. As time goes on there will be new energy sources, but clearly, as those industries evolve, we will continue to see oil and gas being used. Petroleum will be around for at least 50 years longer."[31] Michael Tims of Peters & Co. says, "Suzuki is very dogmatic. Things become difficult to achieve if you have a fixed view and nothing less than your view is acceptable. Progress can be achieved if you have a standard other than the absolute."[32]

Progressive producers are already investing in renewable energy. They know the future of oil is limited and want their companies to survive into the new age. They're expending a great deal of work, thought, and money on plotting scenarios and developing their capacity to make this massive business shift. One example is Suncor, which in early 2000 announced plans to invest up to $100 million by

2005 to develop an alternative- and renewable-energy business. The company wrote a strategic plan and looked at some 700 opportunities for investment. A report says, "In April 2001, Suncor took a major step forward in providing wind power in Canada by partnering with Enbridge Inc. to build a $20 million wind-power project in Gull Lake, Sask." The company says the plant will increase the country's wind-power generation by 10 per cent and be capable of powering about 6,000 homes. Producing the same energy with oil and gas would release about 30,500 tonnes of carbon dioxide a year. Officials of both companies must have been ecstatic when the serendipitous euphony of their two names suggested the obvious catchword: the Sunbridge project.[33] Suncor says that any renewable-energy projects it takes on must reduce greenhouse-gas emissions and not be associated with oil, gas, or coal; require little energy to produce the energy; and have minimum environmental impact. The last criterion is a serious one, because wind-power turbines can maim or kill birds, and the turbines are loud and unsightly. Wind-power proposals are already raising furious objections in some communities. Even the cleanest energy comes with environmental and social cost.

Suncor is also investigating the economics of producing energy from the methane and carbon dioxide produced by landfill sites. All the landfill sites in Canada produce as much greenhouse gas as 6.5 million automobiles. "By capturing these gases, we can reduce these emissions and create an important source of cleaner energy," Suncor says.[34]

Electric utilities are beginning to encourage the use of wind power. In Calgary, Enmax, the city-owned power company, provides a wind-power option for customers willing to pay a premium on their bills. The company uses all the money from that premium to help build windmills and thus add more wind generation to the province's electricity grid. "We can't guarantee you that every electron that comes into your house will originate with wind power," says Enmax spokesman Tony McCallum, "but by supporting our Greenmax program you do encourage wind-power generation."[35] In effect, customers who pay for the option are helping provide wind power for everyone else. Out of the company's 410,000 customers, about 3,000 homeowners and 200 business users paid the premium in 2002.[36]

This is no huge breakthrough, but such measures are at least useful for gauging how much the public is willing to pay for clean energy. A fascinating study by Shell International shows that major shifts in energy sources usually begin with a premium that consumers are increasingly willing to pay.[37] Fifty years ago, heating oil was more costly than coal for home use, but customers were eager to buy it because oil furnaces were so much cleaner and easier to maintain than coal-burning ones. Similarly, natural gas is more expensive today, but once again it's cleaner and easier to deliver than oil. The Kyoto debate has surely heightened demand for clean energy, and the experience at companies like Enmax and Suncor indicates that such projects are becoming viable. The Shell study says, "Because energy costs are a relatively small element in household budgets, paying a premium for such [clean] fuels is widespread in wealthy countries."[38]

Shell pushes its analysis out to the year 2050, speculating that as that date approaches, hydrogen for use in fuel cells will replace oil and gas in pipelines. (Ironically, the initial feedstock for producing hydrogen could only be petroleum.) After that, Shell says, a century-long process of hydrogen infrastructure development will begin. Oil and gas will already be waning because the advantages offered by the new technology will propel the switch to hydrogen well before oil becomes scarce. The higher the demand for fuel cells, the less people will pay for oil. As a result, oil will be cheap enough to be preferred for heat and power in some developing countries but this will not compensate for the declining transport market.[39] And someday, this speculation runs, oil and gas will be as much a part of memory as whale oil.

In the near future, though, oil consumption is expected to rise along with economic growth. This should give energy companies the cushion of prosperity they need to invest heavily in alternative fuels. Those that don't will be the true dinosaurs, because nearly everyone in the industry knows there is no turning back to the days before Kyoto. The debate has heightened public awareness of emissions and their potential dangers. The public clearly expects action and won't tolerate a return to the old ways even if Kyoto fails (still a possibility until countries with 55 percent of emissions ratify). The federal government would need a way to retreat gracefully from the treaty, and the only dignified exit route is through some kind of national or North American program to control emissions. "I don't think anyone disagrees that there's an impact from global warming," says Brian MacNeill, former CEO of Enbridge Inc. "Look at drought problems—there's no doubt the climate has changed. I think what we should be working on is a North American accord."[40]

Eric Newell takes a hard-headed, logical approach. "Whether climate change is human-induced or not, the concentration of greenhouse gas has gone up," he says. "There's lots of evidence to suggest climate change is going on, but I don't get too hung up on the science aspect. It's simply in our interests to reduce our energy use and be as efficient as possible. If global warming isn't there, we have at least saved some money. If it is a disaster, then we have helped save the planet."[41] That pragmatic attitude, very common in the industry, may do more for the environment than all the wind power an army of David Suzukis could muster.

The Challenge

The G-8 Summit meeting held in Calgary on June 26 to 27, 2002, gave globalization protestors their ideal chance to attack choice secondary targets, the national and international oil companies that have their headquarters in the downtown core. Many company executives were worried; they spent on extra security, sent employees home, and kept a nervous eye on the streets. For many Calgarians, there was a whiff of Armageddon in the air, or at least in their minds. They had good reason for trepidation. Some activist groups had hinted at mayhem for months on their Web sites, and several companies had already been victims of bombings and sabotage in the Peace country.

By 7 a.m. on June 26, between 300 and 400 anti–G-8 protestors had gathered at Fort Calgary, on the east side of the downtown core, to snake-march through the city. The goal was to confront global companies and disrupt traffic. Police too were on high alert: Days earlier, a hard core of only 30 radicals had caused havoc at a G-8 finance ministers' meeting in Halifax.

Over the next hour the numbers swelled to 1,500 as the group slowly headed west, then north, then west again. From 8 a.m., the protestors marched south, then west and north. The police grew almost dizzy at the odd route, but they knew why it was happening; radio intercepts at a city command room revealed that the protest leaders were from out of town and didn't know the streets.

Finally their first target was in sight, and within minutes a few protestors were scrambling onto the exterior of the Shell Building, home of petroleum giant Shell Canada.

But the whole affair soon started to look more eccentric than threatening. Among the protestors was a skinny teenage kid in a ladybug get-up complete with a sign that said "G-8, Don't Squish Me." Nobody squished him or anybody else. There was no rock-throwing or stick-swinging by protestors, and no gas-tossing or baton-bashing from police. Soon the protestors abandoned Shell as leaders took the march west and then south. The next destination was McDougall Centre, southern home of the Alberta government. The manicured green lawn looked like an ideal battlefield, but a quick-thinking political gardener hit a button, and suddenly the sprinklers loosed sheets of spray, sending the protestors off to another decadent capitalist destination. But they weren't unhappy with the brief soaking—the temperature was already nearing 25 degrees Celsius.

After 9 a.m. the march moved south and then abruptly east. The Calgary Police Service stopped three anarchists to talk with them. The protestors continued to zigzag past the locked-down Court of Queen's Bench and south to Talisman Energy and Starbucks. The police sent a bike unit to defend these outposts of globalism.

At this point the march was one and a half blocks long. By 9:20 a.m., the quarry was Starbucks, where 30 to 40 protestors stopped briefly before proceeding to Gulf Canada Square, where they and the rest of the marchers were met by the smiling bicycle unit of the Calgary police. Five minutes later, the marchers set off for the next target—could it be the *grande dame* of Calgary hotels, the Fairmont Palliser?

Over the next three hours, the protestors weaved in and out of the downtown, targeting energy prey such as Petro-Canada and

global game such as McDonald's and Starbucks, as well as munici-
pal, provincial, and federal government headquarters. Even as they
broke into their Red, Green, and Black groups and told fellow protestors to remove their contact lenses or put vinegar on their masks,
the marchers were peaceful. Talisman Energy, perennial protest
favourite because of its operations in Sudan, escaped unscathed.
The anti–G-8 protestors made some noise and that was it.

If any city in Canada was to be a target of those who protest oil
(while riding in their cars and fuelling up on fossil remains), it would
surely have to be Calgary, the energy capital of the country. Yet
there was no violent demonstration, no projectiles hurled at their
petroleum prey. Only two protestors were arrested in Calgary all
week, for writing graffiti on rail cars. The outpouring of hatred and
destruction the oil companies feared never came. Executives dared
to imagine that, even among protest groups, they aren't as unpopu-
lar as they'd feared. Industry polls show that all the hard work on
environmental problems is paying off in rising public approval.

Instead of violence at the G-8, there was debate, begun at the
University of Calgary, on globalization, hunger, AIDS, and Kyoto.
Because dialogue and cooperation were favoured over confrontation, these issues sparked lively discussions throughout the land.
The protestors gained respect for their voice, one that had been
lost in the violence of Seattle, Genoa, Washington, and Quebec
City. There seemed also to be a mutual understanding between the
protestors and the police, who in turn earned admiration for their
tolerance and tact.

Yet it would be foolish to assume that protestors and environmentalists have been won over by the industry. Strong concerns
still permeate society over the petroleum industry's relationship
with the environment, and many critics of so-called big oil don't
want to see the change that is taking place. They don't care to
believe that a triple bottom line of economic, social, and environmental responsibility now dominates the best companies in the

oilpatch. The industry is far from perfect, but it does deserve some recognition for making critical changes that continue to improve its environmental performance.

"We've had major environmental improvements in how we do things," says environmental consultant Barry Worbets. "We've gone from huge swaths of D-9 Caterpillars cutting seismic lines to some that are hand-cut and invisible after two months. We've got zero-impact seismic. We've had wholesale improvements over flaring and venting of gas and incredible improvements in technology to reduce emissions. There are major improvements in the quality of gasoline and big benefits in energy efficiency and technical advances. There have been wonderful advances in science and technology. Global positioning systems are used worldwide in environmental tourism and safety and it was all pioneered in Alberta. Alberta's regulation is better, stronger, and more consistent. We have systems in place in Alberta where we try to consult and get people's views. Our systems and society demand a consultative process. The person being impacted does have a say and the ability to change things. The whole consultation with affected stakeholders is done well and the industry is a leader in that."[1]

Despite these obvious achievements, oilpatch leaders point to the need for greater improvements in environmental performance through the next level of technological breakthroughs. They speak of alternative fuel sources, and many want their companies to be the leaders in environmentally friendly energy. These men and women are not enemies of the environment. Certainly many have been prodded and pushed by the public, the shareholders, their employees, their families and friends, but they're finally on board with a grip that is no longer tenuous, but tenacious.

Plenty of work remains to be done. Water use by the industry is a worry for farmers who distrust oil companies, and even for those who rely on the industry for their main "crop"—the cash payments they receive. While a recent study for the Canadian Association of

Petroleum Producers concludes that the industry is not diverting water away from agricultural users, there are those who believe otherwise. The industry must prove to the farming and ranching community that their water sources will not be compromised during all phases of petroleum operations.

"The upstream oil and gas industry certainly recognizes there are public concerns about our use of water," says CAPP vice-president David Pryce. "That is a key reason why we see a trend over the past two decades to continuously improve our use of the resource through recycling, increased use of saline water, greater emphasis on improvements in agricultural areas where others place demands on the water.

"This is a shared resource that benefits many people in many ways. Conventional wisdom or knowledge often fails to recognize current practice and performance and instead portrays water use as unmanaged and irresponsible. An important area for improvement is the actual collection and management of data to help others understand that industry and the regulator have been pro-active in managing the resource."[2]

Pryce says a regulatory approach for water use should build on the existing licensing system for all users. "It should also include basin planning, as well as provide for risk-based planning in the event there are periods when water is in short supply. We believe water-use policy should be based on principles of fairness and sustainable development which balances social, economic, and environmental considerations to the benefit of all Albertans."

The reality is that the petroleum industry holds only about 2.5 per cent of the total licenced water in Alberta and uses only about 60 per cent of that allocation in any given year. Companies that withdraw large amounts are required to recycle over 90 per cent of the produced water.

Water is only one of the issues that concerns CAPP president Pierre Alvarez, who focuses on an array of environmental, social, and economic challenges facing the industry. They include climate change, regulatory reform, land access, tax competitiveness, and Aboriginal concerns. "When industry is overwhelmed by multiple issues and process, it must respond by its best practices," says Alvarez. "The industry is also moving to areas where increasingly the population is Aboriginal and as stakeholders they have issues which are historical and unique."[3]

One of the most important areas for Aboriginal leaders and communities is resolving land claims and honouring historic treaties. The federal government has a critical role to play in allowing First Nations their right to be masters of their land and future. As Eric Newell has pointed out, Aboriginals often have the most innovative of entrepreneurial skills. They deserve to have their voices heard in the symphony of 21st-century developments. Settling land claims establishes the moral and financial framework to encourage Aboriginals into the world of business, but on their terms, on their turf, and in their time. For the federal government, this is an unprecedented opportunity to right historic wrongs. Ottawa has nothing to lose and everything to gain by treating Aboriginal peoples with respect and dignity.

While the industry has made ground-breaking advances in recent years, there is a great deal to be learned and implemented. Veteran lawyer Jerome Slavik believes the industry can build on its best practices by importing and developing ever better ones. "From an economic, financial, and technological point of view to the environment, there are new ways of doing things that gain credibility," he says.[4]

Consider, for example, the building of the northern pipeline. Northwest Territories premier Stephen Kakfwi has made the Aboriginal people's perception abundantly clear 25 years after the Berger Commission: Aboriginal people need the jobs and the Aboriginal communities need the investment and infrastructure. Native cultures can be maintained and fostered even as they secure better houses, better roads, and better systems.

Slavik maintains that if the federal government moved to settle land claims in an expeditious way, it would create significant pools of capital in Aboriginal communities that could help finance industry as well as other ventures. "Government has lots of unfinished business with First Nations in terms of claims. There are 400 to 600 unsettled claims worth between four and six billion dollars. That's why industry should be pushing land-claims settlements. It creates the means by which First Nations can participate with them in their industry."

Too often ideological self-interest guides the kind of advice offered to Natives. First Nations people deserve to have their land claims settled so they can invest in their own businesses, training, and other related programs. With their money, they can decide whether they wish to help develop the oil and gas industry wanting to operate within Aboriginal lands. Ultimately, settling land claims opens the door to Native economic integration. It also extends traditional Native respect for the environment into the petroleum industry. Increasingly, both industry and Aboriginal peoples see the federal and provincial governments as their common barrier to getting things done.

The biggest public-policy problem for the oilpatch is access to land because there's so much activity on it: farming; ranching; general public use; protected areas and parks; hunting and fishing; the industry's own exploring and producing; and the migration of more retirees purchasing small parcels of dreams. As producing regions of the West grow in population, companies face more pressure on the land, more rigorous regulators, more environmental knowledge among the public and industry employees, and more demands for industry action. The modern neighbours of the oilpatch have zero tolerance for emissions, noise, and shoddy practices.

Although oil companies have more difficulty doing business, there are still companies that wouldn't know an innovative strategy if it knocked on the door and planted a kiss. Fortunately, there are also visionaries in the oilpatch, those alchemists who consistently mix creativity, innovation, and financial acumen to create potent industry players. They take the longer view while delicately assuaging the short-term mind of the market.

"It is a long-term relationship," observes Rick George. "What makes our industry unusual is that we have reserves to feed this planet for 50 to a hundred years. Think about how much this industry has changed in just 30 years. And think of the challenges of performing to your stakeholders' expectations, which are going to grow. The demands on you socially, financially, environmentally, and as a leader are all going to be there. We understand our job. And one of our jobs is reducing the environmental impact of every decision we make. A lot of companies have done a really good job there. That gets kind of lost in this polarized environmental debate. But if you take that view that you're going to be in business 50 years from now, then you want to make sure you're doing everything you can do on all those fronts."[5]

That also means working with other industries on common ground to find solutions, something that CAPP and the Alberta government are pursuing. Long-time oilman Jamie Blair, CEO of Exalta Energy and former COO of Husky Energy, would like to see the petroleum and forestry industries fully cooperate in assessing their collective impact in given regions. Currently there isn't enough integration of their information pools on the ecology of areas where they operate. "One of the greatest obstacles to a breakthrough advance in environmental stewardship by the Alberta petroleum industry is the isolation and inaccessibility of advanced ecological databases built over the last 20 years," Blair says. "As a result, individual companies address the ecological impact of their operations with limited information and limited imagination, causing industry to move forward along a linear path designed by history rather than insight and evolution. We need to make dramatic changes to our land-management processes, as current practice too often assumes limitless resources. This assumption may bring us to a very hard end."[6]

The province of Alberta's oil and gas information systems are universally acclaimed. Blair suggests developing freely accessible and comprehensive ecological databases using Alberta's systems as a model. "These systems are the foundation of the most sophisticated oil and gas exploitation industry in the world. Our industry has proven that open access to well, seismic, pipeline, and plant information is the key to efficient development. Imagine the power of such information systems when they are oriented to provide advancements in the way all of society interacts with and impacts ecological systems. Imagine a further step: Include information held external to the industry/academic/scientific community by bringing farmers, trappers, hunters, miners, hikers, and campers into the initiative to pool all of their collective knowledge. Clearly the environment is not an exclusive knowledge domain of scientists."

Just as clearly, environmental respect and protection are not exclusive either. There are passionate environmentalists working within the petroleum industry who want to build land-management systems that reflect the collective intelligence and will of all who interact within the ecosystem. "Alberta has the precedent systems, capital, and education to accomplish such a task and develop a key model for the world to follow," Blair says. "Could we imagine the Alberta oil and gas industry to be the source of an initiative that unleashes the power of information systems to allow the next leap forward in integrated ecological systems thinking?"

If the producer needs to focus on innovation, so does the consumer. Most of the pollution is caused by consumption, and nearly every Canadian adult could save energy by switching habits. Many companies that deliver electricity, like Calgary-based Enmax Energy, offer consumers an option that creates low air pollution—wind power. Other utilities around the country are adopting such programs.

"What is the cost of environmental sustainability?" says veteran industry analyst Martin Molyneaux of FirstEnergy Capital. "The whole environmental issue comes down to what the public is willing to bear, because ultimately those costs are passed through. It can be pushed a lot further if consumers are willing to pay for it.

"What are North American consumers willing to pay for gasoline, diesel, fuel oil? It's a question over which government bodies have to make some difficult decisions but need to be better informed before they make those decisions. It's not good enough to have a great brain trust on the environmental side and equal strength on the corporate side, but with adjudicators in-between who are weak. That's a recipe for disaster. We haven't seen as much progress as we could have made on these issues, because most government levels are not up to the curve. The policy-makers are not helping us. Ultimately consumers have to take responsibility, and up to now, we have not."[7]

It's relatively easy to put an industry on the target range and start shooting when a scapegoat seems useful. What is truly needed is more in-depth research into climate change and environmental sustainability. There is much to be done. Scientists agree that global temperatures have risen about 0.5 degrees Celsius compared to those of a century ago. They also agree that levels of carbon dioxide have moved up over the last two centuries and that its increase will warm the earth—although water vapour and clouds contribute more to earth's warming.

But why is this happening? Scientists differ sharply, despite the claims of Kyoto advocates that there is a universal consensus. "We are not in a position to confidently attribute past climate change to carbon dioxide or to forecast what the climate will be in the future," writes Dr. Richard S. Lindzen in the *Wall Street Journal*.[8]

As one of 11 scientists who released a report on climate change and Kyoto, Dr. Lindzen stated that "there is no consensus, unanimous or otherwise, about long-term climate trends and what causes them . . . [and] that 20 years was too short a period for estimating long-term trends. . . . One reason for this uncertainty is that, as the report states, the climate is always changing; change is the norm."

Dr. Lindzen points to the mini–ice age that the northern hemisphere experienced 200 years ago and the warming trend over the same area a millennium ago. He reminds readers that just 30 years ago, global cooling was the topic of discussion and concern.

"We simply do not know what relation, if any, exists between global climate change and water vapor, clouds, storms, hurricanes and other factors, including regional climate changes, which are generally much larger than global changes and not correlated with them. . . . What we do know is that a doubling of carbon dioxide by itself would produce only a modest temperature increase of one degree Celsius. Larger projected increases depend on 'amplification' of the carbon dioxide by more important, but poorly modeled, greenhouse gases, clouds and water vapour.

"The press has frequently tied the existence of climate change to a need for Kyoto. My own view, consistent with the panel's work, is that the Kyoto Protocol would not result in a substantial reduction in global warming. Given the difficulties in significantly limiting levels of atmospheric carbon dioxide, a more effective policy might well focus on other greenhouse substances whose potential for reducing global warming in a short time may be greater."[9]

Research into global warming and climate change is inconclusive, but many who have political spears to throw grab what they need to thrust their viewpoint at a scientifically naïve public. Dr. Lindzen abhors the use of science "to bludgeon political opponents and propagandize uninformed citizens." He finds it "reprehensible" that patchwork intelligence impedes our understanding of complex issues and "corrodes our ability to make rational decisions."

Nexen vice-president Dr. Randall Gossen feels that Kyoto has everything to do with international trade and nothing to do with the environment, especially given the exclusion of the developing world. Gossen doesn't disagree that action should be taken—but not this kind. "What I would disagree with are the timetables and targets. A 5 or 6 per cent reduction will have no impact, scientifically. What's missing is a clear understanding of the costs associated with the whole climate change issue and how government policy needs to be revised to reflect that reality. What's also missing is a broad understanding by the public of what Kyoto means. This is really a consumer issue."[10]

That is where the focus should be—consumer change. Over the last decade, the industry has reduced carbon emissions per unit of production by 30 per cent while increasing energy efficiency by 30 per cent. It's time to develop public policy that reflects accurate scientific and societal costs, as well as rules that work, rather than trying to fit a square arbitrary date into a round policy hole. Governments should be focusing on things that make economic and environmental sense with regard to reducing CO_2 and methane emissions, rather than rhetoric and fanciful timetables.

As citizens, we can change our lifestyle and conserve energy to the best of our abilities. Are we willing to forego, for example, the fuel-inhaling SUV or using electricity at peak hours? Are we ready to ride the bus or subway to work?

As a global society we need to embrace the next step, which means conserving energy in the highly developed regions of the northern hemisphere. We need to develop efficient and effective energy sources that will help transform the impoverished world into one that can create a reasonable standard of living for its citizens. We should be concentrating on eradicating poverty, hunger, and diseases like AIDS. We need to emulate the technological and environmental successes of petroleum leaders who value ecological sustainability and social responsibility as much as their companies' economic performance. The shift that has happened within the best companies, and finds expression in the mission of CAPP, is a modest but useful model for the world.

Industry leaders bring their social and moral vision to global groups such as the International Petroleum Industry Environmental Conservation Association, where Randall Gossen is chairman. Tremendous technological changes have helped the industry to considerably reduce its impact on the land. "That's the easy part— managing footprints," Gossen says. "The biggest challenge is the social realm. The most effective mechanism for risk management is maintaining strong relationships with every community where you operate. Corporate social responsibility is the right thing to do because it fosters a culture of integrity."

These petroleum leaders promote high moral standards and ethical policies; combat corruption; foster human rights; treat people with dignity and respect; provide an equitable and fair wage; supply social, environmental, and safety expertise; share economic benefits; and value indigenous cultures. "Community investment is more than providing financial and other donations. It's the whole notion of capacity building and transferring social and environmental values as well as technical know-how to communities, including those in host countries where we operate around the world," notes EnCana vice-president Dick Wilson.[11]

The industry is raising the bar by insisting that new members who wish to join its influential Canadian Association of Petroleum Producers must participate in CAPP's environment, health, and safety stewardship program. CAPP's board of directors commanded all current members to sign up for the program by the beginning of 2003. Previously, this was voluntary.

Being environmentally and socially responsible affects the company's bottom line and its stock performance. "More and more questions are coming about ethical funds from the investing constituency," says Molyneaux. "It's not a quantitative thing. It's about who appears to be a leader in environmental responsibility. And that becomes an aspect of my analysis. And it will become a bigger and bigger aspect of the analysis."

This change is fundamental; never before have investment analysts made environmental responsibility a key part of their recommendations to investors. Molyneaux and other influential petroleum analysts such as Wilf Gobert of Peters & Co. recognize how crucial this is to public companies. Cutting emissions costs companies considerable cash and time in the initial stages, but businesses do it to guarantee their future and that of their industry. Producers are finally lining up with strategies similar to the industry leaders, with CAPP providing the blueprint.

"It's good business generally for companies now to address environmental issues as part of their bottom line," adds Peters CEO Michael Tims. "Doing better things for the environment bears a cost, if you don't earn your cost of capital. It all comes down to doing the right thing and earning the return that's appropriate in the circumstances."[12]

The best investment bankers see beyond the next quarter's results. People like Tims, Gobert, Molyneaux, and FirstEnergy chairman Brett Wilson consider themselves protectors of the environment. As Wilson says, "We all have children and this is their future we are creating and protecting, too."[13]

Former finance minister Paul Martin has long admired Canada's oilpatch for its contribution to federal coffers, its business acumen, and its role in reducing its footprint where it operates. "I've found the oil and gas industry to be consistently very understanding and very knowledgeable about the environment," Martin says. "They take a very perceptive and insightful view of the environment."[14] Martin knows the oilpatch as well as, or better than, some federal resource ministers, and took it upon himself to make peace with an industry that distrusted Ottawa after the implementation of the infamous National Energy Program. The NEP took cash out of Western provincial government coffers and bankrupted many companies. When federal health minister Anne McLellan was natural resources minister, she became hugely popular by taking the time to understand the industry. She then introduced the Voluntary Challenge and Registry program that calls on private and public companies and groups to reduce their greenhouse-gas emissions.[15]

As one of the top practitioners in his field, lawyer John Brussa of Burnet, Duckworth & Palmer understands the industry intimately. "The industry is a product of the society it lives in," he says, "and there is probably a much higher level of awareness of environmental concerns as a health issue throughout society, and this has seeped into CEO thinking in the patch."[16]

Brussa believes the oilpatch is more environmentally alert, quick to clean up spills and not poison groundwater. He notes that these are relatively low-cost things to do, but when the costs escalate substantially, he wonders what role the larger society should play.

Brussa calls Kyoto an "unmitigated disaster" because the costs of reducing carbon dioxide on such a massive scale would be huge, and if completely carried by industry could put major parts of it out of business. "It would raise the costs of doing business to an extent that, as we used to say in Catholic school, 'the Mass would no longer be worth the candle.'"

He points out that the Canadian oilpatch is a marginal basin because of its size and cost structure, and that the average rates of return have been quite low. While there are still some large gas discoveries to be made, the average well produces the equivalent of around 50 barrels of oil a day.

"The reason that Alberta is still a viable oil area—like Texas and Oklahoma and other places like that—is that there is political stability, a legal system which is perceived as fair and consistent, and a regulatory burden which takes into account the marginal nature of the production. The only reason that Western Canada has survived as a magnet for capital for the oil industry is by beating down the risk premium—the returns are low, but more certain."

The certainty of those returns is what makes Dick Haskayne bullish about the oilpatch, but worried too. As chairman of TransCanada

PipeLines Ltd. and Fording Inc. as well as a director of Weyerhaeuser Co., Canadian Imperial Bank of Commerce, and EnCana Corp., Haskayne is concerned about Kyoto and the perception of business today, after the unmasking of crooked companies like Enron and WorldCom.

"The business of business that we're in has never had a higher profile, in my opinion, in the 40 years I've been around. At the same time, the reputation of business has never been lower. The standard of business conduct and ethics has been shameful."[17] Haskayne made those remarks when he and his wife, Lois, donated $16 million to the University of Calgary's school of business. Haskayne noted that everyone has to work to change flawed management approaches and strategies, especially business schools. Haskayne lashed out at excessive executive pay and bonuses, accounting hijinks, and questionable corporate governance.

"I expect Dick Haskayne had no idea how prescient his words would be when he took local and national corporate leaders to task this week for failing to create an ethical and moral business climate Canadians can be proud of," wrote Charles Frank, business editor of the *Calgary Herald*. "Whether it is senior executives taking million-dollar bonuses while their company's fortunes are plummeting, companies 'gaming' emerging power markets in search of untold millions, or investment advisors touting firms in which their employer had a potential vested interest from underwriting fees . . . it all adds up to the same thing: a disturbing decline in corporate morals—and a corresponding plunge in consumer and investor confidence."[18]

Calgary Herald columnist Scott Haggett hoped that satire would get the message across to corrupt managers and businesses. "Finally we're getting star billing," he wrote after WorldCom Inc.'s former CEO, Bernard Ebbers, resigned once the U.S. Securities and Exchange Commission looked into the company's accounting practices. WorldCom appeared to have loaned Ebbers, a Canadian raised in

Edmonton, about US $408 million. "After years of being in a leadership position when it comes to corporate scandals—think Bre-X Minerals Ltd., VisuaLabs Inc., YBM Magnex International Inc.— Canada was in imminent danger of falling well behind in the race to the bottom," Haggett wrote.[19]

Scandals are suffocating business ethics and few industries are immune to the greed and venality of corporate executives who can't get enough. Rules are for lowly employees to follow; senior executives make their own. This is the malaise that threatens capitalism far more than communism ever did.

The leaders in the oilpatch are as acutely aware of the ethics challenge as they are of the environmental one. "For whatever reason, many companies are increasingly holding themselves to a higher standard, and yet many of our critics see no reason to hold themselves to that same high standard," says Shell senior vice-president Ray Woods.[20] Woods also acknowledges that there are petroleum companies whose standard of integrity can be pretty low. Those companies must be brought to the environmental starting gate and given a whack. As CAPP president Pierre Alvarez says, "The unfortunate reality is that industry is often judged by the worst offender, not by the best practitioner."

The values of a corporation are a critical element in attracting the best talent. "What you stand for does matter," says Suncor vice-president Gordon Lambert. "We've seen it with our entry into the renewable-energy field. People want to work for a company that is doing good things and looking at energy broadly."[21]

Environmental activist Martha Kostuch wants Western petroleum leaders, like Alberta, to turn away from fossil fuels toward new energy sources. "We're just becoming more efficient polluters," she says. "Earth is a spaceship and we're fouling it up. Technology alone is not the answer. This is much bigger than technology. It is a lifestyle. Energy consumption per home is up. People are building bigger homes and using more appliances. It's a question of fairness and equity here."[22]

Yet Canada also operates in an intensely competitive international environment. If our production and exports are cut back for environmental reasons, the need will likely be supplied by others, with worse environmental effects. "Venezuela and Mexico will ramp up and fill the demand," says CAPP president Pierre Alvarez. "Will that help?" It certainly won't, because their production isn't as clean and technically advanced as that of Canada.

The argument cuts no ice with Kostuch. "That's like saying if we don't supply heroin, then someone else will. That's a really bad excuse. Do we want to go to the top of the barrel and compare ourselves to Denmark, or be on the bottom of the barrel and compare ourselves with Venezuela?"

One of the industry's greatest recent achievements is that it has learned to talk to people like Kostuch, and even learn a great deal from them. In order to convince the public that they've improved, oil and gas companies make a running start when they can form a strategic alliance with sincere and reasonable critics. Always wary and skeptical, Kostuch nonetheless concedes that some companies have made great progress. David Pryce has worked well with her by participating in groups like CASA and finding common ground. "We can really attain some successes," he says. "They aren't always what we anticipated. We ask what the barriers are to getting good solutions and then the solutions can end up better than either of us expected and be quite workable. There are some pretty dedicated folks in the trenches in industry, government, and elsewhere who are looking for solutions."[23]

Yet there remains a strange dichotomy in the Canadian public's attitude toward the industry. This is partly regional politics: Petroleum helps propel Alberta, Saskatchewan, and B.C., as well as the North and the Atlantic Provinces. But the two most populous and politically powerful provinces, Ontario and Quebec, don't have oil and gas, so most people in those provinces are only dimly aware of the industry's many benefits to their economies. "I don't think the people in Ontario see themselves as beneficiaries of the oil industry when in many respects they are," says Dr. Roger Gibbins, president of the respected Canada West Foundation.[24] For example, when a dollar is spent on the Alberta oilsands, 27 cents goes to Ontario and 19 cents to Quebec, mostly to purchase equipment.

But the industry is easy to beat up on because, although it's essential (more than 3,000 products are derived from petroleum), it is far from glamorous. Nobody thinks about oil and gas when they take a painkiller, play a compact disc, pull on a fleece vest, put vegetables in a plastic refrigerator bag, use a toothbrush, or employ hundreds of other items that are made from petroleum or contain something made from petroleum. Few people ever envision the industry's huge contribution to employment, investment, technology, and Canada's balance of trade. But they're always ready to fume when they feel they're getting ripped off at the gasoline pumps or hear attacks on pollution based on practices that haven't been used for many years.

EnCana's Gwyn Morgan caught the contradictions in a speech to the 2002 Canadian Newspapers Conference.

"For something so intrinsic to our lives, there remains a strange love-hate relationship," he said. "We love to use it, but we hate to pay for it. We know we need to find, produce, transport, and process it, but don't want that happening anywhere near us. We love to drive our SUVs, but we hate to fill them up. We love a warm, cozy home, but we hate to pay the gas bill. We love to banish our child's infection with a sulphur-based drug, but we hate to go near a sour gas plant."[25]

Yet Morgan noted that at a deeper everyday level, people depend on and trust oil and gas companies to get the job done. "You've trusted the industry to continually fuel the very workings of our society, to continue to produce petroleum indefinitely," he said. "You take for granted that you will always have the energy you need." One reason for this is that Canada's industry is the safest in the world, routinely drilling without incident in tricky places like the *Perfect Storm* seas off the east coast. These daily achievements aren't always recognized, Morgan feels, because the industry has usually taken a "hot-button" approach rather than following the example of forestry and providing Canadians with facts about its achievements over the long term.

Like many industry leaders, Morgan feels that the business will have a great deal to boast about as the years go by. "People will more and more realize that it is one of the highest-technology industries in the world," he says. "Producing oil and gas will have less and less impact on the environment." New technologies on the consuming end will cut air pollution to the point where it's no longer an issue, he feels. Producers will continue to hire some of the best environmentalists as powerful forces within their companies, and make social contribution part of their corporate mantra.

To an oil industry employee who had his or her last sight of the industry 25 years ago, all these improvements would appear so alien as to seem impossible. The best executives are determined that today's retiring employee, offered a glimpse of the future as many years hence, will have exactly the same feeling. The oil and gas industry has changed vastly for the better, and nobody wants to go back.

Notes

CHAPTER ONE   The Patch

1. Jim Boucher interview, May 1, 2002.
2. Joyce Metchewais interview, April 24, 2001.
3. Jerome Slavik interview, April 11, 2002.
4. Gordon Lambert interview, April 16, 2002.
5. Rick George interview, April 11, 2002.
6. Figures provided by the Canadian Association of Petroleum Producers (CAPP).
7. Stephen Kakfwi speech to the annual CAPP dinner, April 18, 2002.
8. Martha Kostuch interview, April 12, 2002.
9. Greta Raymond interview, April 1, 2002.
10. See "Canada won't decide on Kyoto by Earth Summit," by Randall Palmer of Reuters in *Financial Post*, August 10, 2002, p. FP8.
11. Charlie Fischer interview, May 1, 2002.
12. Energy Information Administration. Canada: Environmental Issues. Accessed April 11, 2002. http://www.eia.doe.gov/cabs/canenv.html.
13. See "Canadians told to park their SUVs: German joins in criticism of accord stance," by Tom Maloney in *Calgary Herald*, April 15, 2002, p. A1.
14. Murray Edwards interview, March 14, 2002.

CHAPTER TWO   The Shift

1. Gwyn Morgan interview, April 29, 2002.
2. George Govier interview, April 30, 2002.
3. Jeff Jones interview, May 14, 2002.
4. Wilf Gobert interview, April 3, 2002.
5. Rick George interview, April 11, 2002.
6. Discussion with Alejandro Suarez, Ecuadorian ambassador to Canada, April 23, 2002.
7. Charlie Fischer interview, May 1, 2002.
8. Gordon Lambert interview, April 16, 2002.
9. Kathy Sendall interview, May 27, 2002.
10. Brian MacNeill interview, April 12, 2002.
11. Irene Pfeiffer interview, May 21, 2002.
12. David Pryce interview, March 5, 2002.
13. David Pryce correspondence to author, July 15, 2002.
14. Pierre Alvarez interview, April 4, 2002.
15. Eric Newell interview, April 2, 2002.
16. See the Dow Jones Web site, www.sustainabilityindex.com/faq.html.
17. Hazel Gillespie interview, April 1, 2002.
18. Dick Wilson interview, June 4, 2002.
19. Joyce Metchewais interview, April 24, 2001.
20. Barbara Zach interview, April 3, 2002.
21. Bjorn Lomborg, *The Skeptical Environmentalist: Measuring the Real State of the World* (Cambridge: Cambridge University Press, 2001), p. 192.
22. Ibid., p. 194.
23. See www.corpwatch.org.campaigns/PCD.jsp/articleid=218.
24. See *Oilweek*, March 4, 2002.
25. Eric Newell interview, April 18, 2002.
26. Martha Kostuch interview, March 27, 2002.
27. Barry Worbets interview, April 26, 2002.
28. Elaine McCoy interview, April 15, 2002.
29. Tom Marr-Laing interview, May 9, 2002.
30. Tim Faithfull, in Shell Canada's 11th annual *Sustainable Development Report*, May 21, 2002.
31. Ray Woods interview, April 18, 2002.
32. Murray Edwards interview, March 14, 2002.

CHAPTER THREE   The Outlaw

1. During the late 1970s and early 1980s I examined and wrote about the role of women and men on the frontier, focusing on the Peace River area. I lived in Beaverlodge, Alberta, and researched the farming community in Goodfare, near Hythe, where Wiebo Ludwig and his clan now live. I also interviewed Natives at the Horse Lake reserve. In addition, my family lived in Grande Prairie for nearly a decade.

2. C.A. Dawson, unpublished notes (Edmonton: University of Alberta Bruce Peel Special Collections), Book I, p. 131.

3. Dawson, unpublished notes, Book I, p. 93.

4. Dawn Faris, "The Effect of Social and Technological Change upon the Role of the Housewife in the Peace River Country." Unpublished paper, 1968.

5. Dawson, unpublished notes, Book I, p. 131.

6. Dawson's notes are intriguing reading for anyone with an interest in the history of the Peace River area and the personalities of the people who came to farm on the frontiers of settlement. Also see C.A. Dawson and R.W. Murchie, *The Settlement of the Peace River Country: A Study of a Pioneer Area* (Toronto: Macmillan, 1934) and C.A. Dawson and Eva R. Younge, *Pioneering in the Prairie Provinces: The Social Side of Settlement Process* (Toronto: Macmillan, 1940).

7. Faris captures this in her paper, p. 16.

8. Ibid., p. 12.

9. See David Staples, "A harsh shepherd: Of faith and fury," *Edmonton Journal*, December 11, 1999, and "Trouble at Trickle Creek," *Edmonton Journal*, December 12, 1999.

10. Mark Levine, "The Souring of the Good Reverend's Nature," *Outside Magazine*, December 1998, p. 112.

11. Rob Everton interview, April 18, 2002.

12. Dymphny Dronyk interview, July 16, 2002. Dronyk first made the point in the *National Post*. See note 13.

13. Christie Blatchford, "Wiebo's dynamite," *National Post*, April 8, 2000.

14. This occurred on September 14, 1998, outside the Metropolitan Centre in Calgary, where Ludwig was holding a news conference in response to the one held inside by Gwyn Morgan, then CEO of Alberta Energy Co. Morgan was discussing the bombings and fear in the Peace River area and the concerns of the community.

15. Dronyk detailed the behaviour in our interview. She also discussed this with Christie Blatchford, who reported it in her April 8 piece.
16. Dronyk interview with author.
17. Ibid.
18. Blatchford, "Wiebo's dynamite."
19. Levine, *Outside Magazine*, p. 173.
20. Sydney Sharpe, "Page Two" column, *Calgary Sun*, January 17, 1999.
21. Brian Peterson interview, April 22, 2002.
22. Gwyn Morgan interview, April 29, 2002.
23. Brian Bergman, "Disturbing the Peace," *Maclean's*, February 8, 1999.
24. Correspondence with Greg Gilbertson of the EUB, June 3, 2002.
25. Gisela Everton interview, April 18, 2002.
26. Rob Everton interview, June 14, 2002.
27. Government of Alberta Health and Wellness, news release, May 23, 2002.
28. Study fact sheet, May 23, 2002.
29. As indeed did my father, Paul Sharpe, with his family witnessing his reading.
30. Wiebo Ludwig interview, June 22, 1999. Also see Sydney Sharpe, "Page Two" column, *Calgary Sun*, June 23, 1999.
31. Gisela Everton interview, June 22, 1999.
32. Andrew Nikiforuk, *Saboteurs: Wiebo Ludwig's War Against Big Oil* (Toronto: Macfarlane Walter and Ross, 2001), p. 233.
33. Nikiforuk, *Saboteurs*.
34. Tahnis Petterson interview, May 2, 2002.
35. John Petterson interview, May 2, 2002.
36. Transcript from the funeral of Karman Willis.
37. Gwyn Morgan interview, April 29, 2002.
38. Randall Gossen interview, April 2, 2002.

CHAPTER FOUR The Talk

1. Barry Worbets interview, April 8, 2002.
2. Brian Bietz interview, April 9, 2002.
3. Vivian Pharis strongly supported the nomination of Barry Worbets for the Emerald Award with a lengthy and passionate statement.
4. Tom Beck also supported Worbets for the Emerald Award.

5. Martha Kostuch interview, April 12, 2002.

6. Kathy Sendall interview, May 27, 2002.

7. Gwyn Morgan interview, April 29, 2002.

8. Bill Clapperton interview, April 1, 2002.

9. David Pryce interview, March 5, 2002.

10. Rick George interview, April 11, 2002.

11. Charlie Fischer interview, May 1, 2002.

12. Tom Marr-Laing interview, May 9, 2002.

13. See the CAPP "2001 Environment, Health and Safety Stewardship Progress Report," p. 1.

14. Brian Bietz interview, April 9, 2002.

15. Murray Edwards interview, March 14, 2002.

16. See Anne George, "Age of Distrust," *Oilweek*, March 2002, pp. 36–39.

17. See the Petroleum Communication Foundation's study in its *Connexions* newsletter, Fall 1999.

18. Gary Webster interview, March 18, 2002.

19. Roger Gibbins interview, March 12, 2002.

20. Brian Bietz interview, March 21, 2002.

21. Charlie Fischer interview, May 1, 2002.

22. Jerome Slavik interview, April 11, 2002.

23. Jim Boucher interview, May 1, 2002.

24. Martha Kostuch interview, March 27, 2002.

25. Martha Kostuch interview, April 12, 2002.

26. Eric Newell interview, April 2, 2002.

27. Martha Kostuch interview, March 27, 2002.

28. Greta Raymond interview, April 1, 2002.

29. Eric Newell interview, April 18, 2002.

30. Eric Newell interview, April 2, 2002.

31. Rick George interview, April 11, 2002.

32. Gordon Lambert interview, April 16, 2002.

33. Brian MacNeill interview, April 12, 2002.

34. Ray Woods interview, April 18, 2002.

35. Michael Tims interview, April 3, 2002.

36. Dean Lien interview, May 1, 2002.

37. Canadian Association of Petroleum Producers (CAPP) and Small Explorers and Producers Association of Canada (SEPAC), "Action on Energy: A Progress Report from Alberta's Oil and Gas Industry," 2001.

38. CAPP and SEPAC, "Action on Energy."

39. Frank Dabbs interview, March 21, 2002.
40. Hydrogeological Consultants Ltd., "Use of Water by the Upstream Oil and Gas Industry." A study prepared for the Canadian Association of Petroleum Producers, March 2002. Also see Tony Seskus, "Oil industry using too much water, farmers say," *Financial Post*, August 10, 2002, and Mark Lowey, "Oilpatch and agriculture in water fight," *Business Edge*, August 22–September 4, 2002.
41. Gary Sargent interview, March 25, 2002.
42. Gordon Jaremko interview, March 20, 2002.
43. CAPP vice-president David Pryce correspondence, July 15, 2002.
44. Excerpted from a review by Andrea Lorenz, "Ambassadors of Industry," *Oilweek*, May 6, 2002.
45. See Dr. Waldner's remarks in Robert Bott, "Sour Gas, Questions + Answers," Petroleum Communications Foundation, October 2000, p. 30.
46. Bott, "Sour Gas, Questions + Answers," p. 31.
47. Western Interprovincial Scientific Studies Association news release, November 19, 2001.
48. Michael O'Connell interview, April 24, 2002.
49. Peter Lougheed interview, April 15, 2002.
50. See the Canadian Association of Petroleum Producers, "2001 Environment, Health and Safety Stewardship Progress Report," p. 14.
51. Simone Marler interview, March 18, 2002.

CHAPTER FIVE   The Rules

1. Neil McCrank interview, March 26, 2002.
2. Greg Gilbertson (Alberta Energy and Utilities Board) interview, May 14, 2002.
3. Ibid.
4. Gwyn Morgan interview, April 29, 2002.
5. Kim Eastlick interview, March 25, 2002.
6. The Appropriate Dispute Resolution (ADR) program is explained in an EUB informational letter dated January 8, 2001. The ADR outlines "a range of dispute resolution mechanisms" as well as a "traditional EUB hearing." It's available on-line at http://www.eub.gov.ab.ca/bbs/ils/ils/il2001-01.htm.
7. EUB Web site, p. 3.

8. EUB Web site, p. 7.

9. Gilbertson interview, May 14, 2002.

10. Brian Bietz interview, March 21, 2002.

11. Debbie Taras interview, May 23, 2002.

12. Martin Molyneaux interview, April 18, 2002.

13. David Breen, *Alberta's Petroleum Industry and the Conservation Board* (Edmonton: University of Alberta Press, 1993). Dr. Breen is a noted historian; his book is the most comprehensive analysis of the industry and the politics behind Alberta's regulatory bodies.

14. For example, the Markin Flanagan Writer-in-Residence Program at the University of Calgary is nationally regarded. Flanagan is also the creator and publisher of *AlbertaViews*, a respected liberal voice in Alberta, considered by many to be an alternative to *Alberta Report* magazine.

15. Al Markin interview, March 21, 2002.

16. George Govier interview, April 30, 2002.

17. Peter Lougheed interview, April 15, 2002.

18. Breen, *Alberta's Petroleum Industry*, p. 267.

19. Govier interview.

20. David Pryce interview, March 5, 2002.

21. EUB, Provincial Advisory Committee on Public Safety and Sour Gas, Final Recommendations and Appendices, p. 1.

22. See, for example, the EUB Public Safety and Sour Gas Implementation Plan Quarterly Progress Report, October 26, 2001. Check the on-line site: http://www.eub.gov.ab.ca.

23. See Chapter 6.

24. EUB Guide 60—A Sneak Preview, May 12, 2002.

25. Eastlick interview.

26. Martha Kostuch interview, April 12, 2002.

27. EUB General Bulletin 2002–05.

28. Kim Eastlick correspondence, May 28, 2002.

29. Gary Webster interview, March 18, 2002.

30. Tom Marr-Laing interview, May 9, 2002.

31. EUB, "Upstream Petroleum Industry Flaring Report," Statistical Series 2001–60B, July 2001, p. 1.

32. EUB, "Upstream Petroleum Industry Flaring Report."

33. Patricia Gariepy Leeson interview, May 21, 2002.

34. Webster interview.

35. Breen, *Alberta's Petroleum Industry*, p. xix. In particular, Breen takes to task John Richards and Larry Pratt, *Prairie Capitalism: Power and Influence in the New West* (Toronto: McClelland and Stewart, 1979) and Alvin Finkel, *The Social Credit Phenomenon in Alberta* (Toronto: University of Toronto Press, 1989).
36. Ibid., p. 678, n. 5.
37. Hydrogeological Consultants Ltd., "Use of Water by the Upstream Oil-and-gas Industry." Study prepared for the Canadian Association of Petroleum Producers, March 2002, p. 5.
38. Ibid., p. 30.
39. Jerome Slavik interview, April 11, 2002.
40. "First Nations Issues." Presentation to the Canadian Association of Petroleum Producers' Board of Directors, March 20, 2002.
41. See the *Sparrow* decision on the Nisga'a on-line site at http://www.ntc.bc.ca/no_frames/sparrow.html.
42. Wilf Gobert interview, April 3, 2002.
43. Dan MacLennan interview, April 22, 2002.
44. Gordon Jaremko interview, March 20, 2002.
45. Jaremko, *Oilweek*, March 2000.
46. Rick George interview, April 11, 2002.

CHAPTER SIX The Tools

1. Peter McKenzie-Brown, Gordon Jaremko, and David Finch, *The Great Oil Age* (Calgary: Detselig Enterprises Ltd., 1993), p. 153.
2. Robert Bott, "Sour Gas: Questions + Answers," Petroleum Communication Foundation, October 2000, p. 15.
3. The author had access to a number of emergency response plans, and also discussed their requirements with environmental consultant Barry Worbets.
4. Bott, "Sour Gas: Questions + Answers."
5. See John R. Webber, *Hydrogen Sulfide Safety Basics* (Sherwood Park, Alberta: Pacific Safety Institute, 2000). Also see *Workplace Health & Safety: Hydrogen Sulphide* (Edmonton: Alberta Human Resources and Employment, July 1998); H_2S: *"The Killer"* (Edmonton: Alberta Occupational Health and Safety, 1988); Alberta *Occupational Health*

and Safety Act (O-2 RSA 2000); Chemical Hazards Regulation (Alberta Regulation 393/88), *Occupational Health and Safety Act*.

6. Bott, "Sour Gas: Questions + Answers," p. 14.
7. *Oilweek*, May 6, 2002, p. 28.
8. Fred Stenson, *Waste to Wealth: A History of Gas Processing in Canada* (Calgary: Canadian Gas Processors Association, 1985), pp. 267–68.
9. Gordon Jaremko interview, March 20, 2002.
10. Canadian Association of Petroleum Producers (CAPP) and Small Explorers and Producers Association of Canada (SEPAC), "Action on Energy: A Progress Report from Alberta's Oil and Gas Industry," 2001.
11. Melanie Collison, "Sore Spot," *Oilweek*, March 4, 2002, p. 32.
12. See the CASA Web site at http://www.casahome.org/.
13. John Squarek interview, June 6, 2002.
14. Gwyn Morgan interview, April 29, 2002.
15. David Pryce interview, March 5, 2002.
16. Robert Bott, *Our Petroleum Challenge* (Calgary: Petroleum Communications Foundation, 1999), p. 45.
17. Eric Newell interview, April 2, 2002.
18. Rick George interview, April 11, 2002.
19. Gordon Lambert interview, April 16, 2002.
20. Brian Bietz interview, April 9, 2002.
21. Brian MacNeill interview, April 12, 2002.
22. Stenson, *Waste to Wealth*, pp. 297–98.
23. Reprinted in David Breen, *Alberta's Petroleum Industry and the Conservation Board* (Edmonton: University of Alberta Press, 1993), p. 51.
24. Frank Dabbs interview, March 21, 2002.
25. Greta Raymond interview, April 1, 2002.
26. Tom Marr-Laing interview, May 9, 2002.
27. Barry Worbets interview, April 4, 2002.
28. Michael Tims interview, April 3, 2002.
29. Bill Clapperton interview, April 1, 2002.
30. Martha Kostuch interview, April 12, 2002.
31. Tim Faithfull, *Progress Toward Sustainable Development—2000 Sustainable Development Report Summary* (Calgary: Shell, April 2000).
32. Ibid., p. 6.
33. Ron Brenneman, *Petro-Canada Report to the Community* (Calgary: Petro-Canada, no date).

34. Charlie Fischer and Randall Gossen, Nexen Inc. *Safety, Environment & Social Responsibility—Annual Report 2001* (Calgary: Nexen, February 7, 2002).
35. *Alberta Energy Company Corporate Constitution* (Calgary: AEC, June 4, 2001).
36. Gwyn Morgan, "A Canadian Global Champion—Welcome Address to Employees of EnCana Corporation," Calgary, April 8, 2002.

CHAPTER SEVEN The Accord

1. For analysis of regional factors, see Don Braid and Sydney Sharpe, *Breakup: Why the West Feels Left out of Canada* (Toronto: Key Porter Books, 1990) and Sydney Sharpe and Don Braid, *Storming Babylon: Preston Manning and the Rise of the Reform Party* (Toronto: Key Porter Books, 1992).
2. See Greenpeace Web site at http://www.greenpeace.org and the Canadian affiliate at http://www.greenpeace.ca/e/index.php.
3. See the Research Branch of Agriculture and Agri-Food Canada Web site at http://res2.agr.gc.ca/research-recherche/science/Healthy_Air/2c.html.
4. Diane Francis, "Kyoto Accord a bad deal for Canada: Emissions pact commitment should match Australia's," *Financial Post*, March 12, 2002.
5. See the David Suzuki Foundation Web site at http://www.davidsuzuki.org/.
6. Ibid.
7. For a large selection of government documents related to climate change, follow the links at the Web site "Sustaining the Environment" at http://www.environmentandresources.ca/.
8. Associated Press, "Australia refuses to ratify Kyoto Accord," *Calgary Herald*, June 6, 2002.
9. For full terms of the Protocol and many other related documents, see "United Nations Framework on Climate Change" at the United Nations Web site: http://unfccc.int/index.html.
10. Allan MacRae, "Reject the Kyoto scam," *National Post*, August 1, 2002.
11. Peter Lougheed interview, April 15, 2002.
12. Don Braid, "Lougheed urges Kyoto fight," *Calgary Herald*, September 1, 2002.
13. Eric Beauchesne, "Transfers to have-nots neutralize oil advantage," *National Post*, August 1, 2002.

14. Scott Haggett, "Alberta on brink of energy showdown," *Calgary Herald*, May 23, 2002.

15. David G. Wood, *The Lougheed Legacy* (Toronto: Key Porter Books, 1985), pp. 173–78.

16. Eric Newell interview, April 2, 2002.

17. Peter Menzies, "Kyoto myths cloud debate," *Calgary Herald*, June 6, 2002.

18. Chris Varcoe, "Abandon Kyoto CEOs urge," *Calgary Herald*, June 21, 2002.

19. Peter Lougheed interview, August 31, 2002.

20. Grant Patrick e-mail correspondence with the author, June 16, 2002.

21. See Kyodo News on the Web, "Japan Ratifies Kyoto Protocol," Tokyo, June 4, 2002 at http://home.kyodo.co.jp/.

22. "Kyoto to be ratified in fall: MP," *National Post*, August 20, 2002.

23. "Global Warming: The Origin and Nature of the Alleged Scientific Consensus," by Dr. Richard S. Lindzen, Alfred P. Sloan Professor of Meteorology at the Massachusetts Institute of Technology, published in the *Cato Review of Business & Government*, 1992, v. 15, no. 2.

24. Steven Chase and Heather Scoffield, "Canada develops alternatives to Kyoto, Rock says," *Globe and Mail*, May 7, 2002.

25. Alan Toulin, "Environment key part of power equation," *National Post*, June 18, 2002.

26. Braid, "Lougheed urges Kyoto fight."

27. See the report "Perspective on Climate Change," April 2002, on the Institute's Web site at http://www.pembina.org/.

28. Ibid.

29. Pembina Institute, "Comparison of Current Government Action on Climate Change in the U.S. and Canada," May 2002.

30. Ibid.

31. Gary Webster interview, March 18, 2002.

32. Michael Tims interview, April 3, 2002.

33. Cited in Suncor's 2001 report on sustainability, "Our Journey Toward Sustainable Development."

34. Ibid.

35. Tony McCallum interview, June 15, 2002.

36. Ibid.

37. Shell International, "Energy Needs, Choices and Responsibilities."

38. Ibid.

39. Ibid.

40. Brian MacNeill interview, April 12, 2002.
41. Eric Newell interview, April 2, 2002.

CHAPTER EIGHT   The Challenge

1. Barry Worbets interview, April 4, 2002.
2. David Pryce correspondence, July 4, 2002.
3. Pierre Alvarez interview, April 4, 2002.
4. Jerome Slavik interview, April 11, 2002.
5. Rick George interview, April 11, 2002.
6. Jamie Blair interview, June 25, 2002.
7. Martin Molyneaux interview, April 18, 2002.
8. Dr. Richard S. Lindzen's column appeared in the editorial pages of the *Wall Street Journal*, June 11, 2001.
9. Dr. Lindzen's testimony before the U.S. Senate Environment and Public Works Committee on May 2, 2001, is available at this Web site: http://www/senate.gov/~epw/lin_0502.htm.
10. Randall Gossen interview, April 2, 2002.
11. Dick Wilson interview, June 4, 2002.
12. Michael Tims interview, April 3, 2002.
13. Brett Wilson interview, April 16, 2002.
14. Paul Martin interview, July 6, 2002.
15. The success of the VCR program is seen on its Web site at http://www.vcr-mvr.ca/home_e.cfm.
16. John Brussa correspondence, July 7, 2002.
17. Dick Haskayne speech at the University of Calgary on May 28, 2002. Also personal interview.
18. Charles Frank, "Ethical issues bubble over," *Calgary Herald*, May 31, 2002.
19. Scott Haggett, "A world-class contribution to business," *Calgary Herald*, July 3, 2002.
20. Ray Woods interview, April 18, 2002.
21. Gordon Lambert interview, April 16, 2002.
22. Martha Kostuch interview, April 12, 2002.
23. David Pryce interview, May 8, 2002.
24. Roger Gibbins interview, March 12, 2002.
25. Gwyn Morgan, "Remarks to the Canadian Newspapers Super Conference Panel Discussion," Calgary, April 25, 2002.

Bibliography

Booklets, Pamphlets, and Brochures

Alberta Ecotrust. *Connecting*. Newsletter of the Alberta Ecotrust Foundation. Issue No. 9, June 2001.

Alberta Energy Company (AEC). *AEC: Partner of Choice*. Corporate brochure. Calgary: AEC, no date.

Altus Environmental Engineering Ltd. *Climate Change Success Stories*. Calgary: Canadian Association of Petroleum Producers, 2001.

Bott, Robert. *Our Petroleum Challenge: Exploring Canada's Oil and Gas Industry*. Sixth Edition. Calgary: Petroleum Communication Foundation, 1999.

———. *Flaring: Questions + Answers*. Calgary: Petroleum Communication Foundation, 2000.

———. *Sour Gas: Questions + Answers*. Calgary: Petroleum Communication Foundation, 2000.

Canadian Association of Petroleum Producers (CAPP). *2001 Report to Members*. Calgary, Halifax, St. John's: CAPP, 2001.

———. *Drilling an Offshore Well in Atlantic Canada*. Calgary, Halifax, St. John's: CAPP, 2001.

———. *Emergency Planning and Response: Protecting People and the Environment in the Offshore Oil and Gas Industry*. Calgary, Halifax, St. John's: CAPP, 2001.

———. *Health and Safety in the Offshore Oil and Gas Industry in Atlantic Canada*. Calgary, Halifax, St. John's: CAPP, 2001.

———. *Milestones in Canada's National Petroleum Industry*. Calgary: CAPP, no date.

———. *Offshore Drilling Rigs*. Calgary, Halifax, St. John's: CAPP, 2001.

———. *Oil + Natural Gas*. Brochure. Calgary: CAPP, April 2001.

———. *Outlook for the Natural Gas Industry in Atlantic Canada*. Calgary, Halifax, St. John's: CAPP, 2001.

———. *Producing Oil and Gas Offshore*. Calgary, Halifax, St. John's: CAPP, 2001.

———. *Seismic Surveys: The Search for Oil and Gas in Offshore Atlantic Canada*. Calgary, Halifax, St. John's: CAPP, 2001.

———. *Transportation of Oil and Gas from the Atlantic Offshore to Market*. Calgary, Halifax, St. John's: CAPP, 2001.

International Petroleum Industry Environmental Conservation Association (IPIECA). *IPIECA in Profile*. Corporate brochure. London: IPIECA, October 2001.

Nexen Inc. *International Code of Ethics for Canadian Business*. Calgary: Nexen, no date.

———. *Nexen—Energy to Outperform*. Calgary: Nexen, no date.

Petroleum Communication Foundation (PCF). *Connexions, A Newsletter for Members and the Public*. Calgary: PCF, Fall 1999.

———. *Connexions, A Newsletter for Members and the Public*. Issue 3. Calgary: PCF, 2001.

Shell Canada Limited. *Listening and Responding—Action Today with Tomorrow in Mind*. Calgary: Shell, no date.

———. *Progress Toward Sustainable Development—2000 Sustainable Development Report Summary*. Calgary: Shell, April 2001.

Shell International Ltd. *Energy Needs, Choices and Possibilities: Scenarios to 2050*. Pamphlet. London: Royal Dutch/Shell Group of Companies, March 10, 2001.

Suncor Energy Inc. *Our Journey Toward Sustainable Development—A Summary of the 2001 Report on Sustainability*. Calgary: Suncor, September 2001.

Webber, John R. *Hydrogen Sulfide Safety Basics*. Sherwood Park, Alberta: Pacific Safety Institute, 2000.

Books

Binnie-Clark, Georgina. *Wheat and Women*. 1914, reprint. Toronto: University of Toronto Press, 1979.

Boustie, Sylvie, Marlo Raynolds, and Matthew Bramley. *How Ratifying the Kyoto Protocol Will Benefit Canada's Competitiveness*. Drayton Valley, Alberta: Pembina Institute, June 2002.

Bowes, Gordon E., editor. *Peace River Chronicles*. Vancouver: Prescott Publishing Co., 1963.

Braid, Don, and Sydney Sharpe. *Breakup: Why the West Feels Left Out of Canada*. Toronto: Key Porter Books, 1990.

Bramley, Matthew. *A Comparison of Current Government Action on Climate Change in the U.S. and Canada*. Drayton Valley: Pembina Institute, May 2002.

Breen, David H. *Alberta's Petroleum Industry and the Conservation Board*. Edmonton: University of Alberta Press, 1993.

Dawson, C.A., and Eva R. Younge. *Pioneering in the Prairie Provinces: The Social Side of Settlement Process.* Toronto: Macmillan, 1940.

Dawson, C.A., and R.W. Murchie. *The Settlement of the Peace River Country: A Study of a Pioneer Area.* Toronto: Macmillan, 1934.

Fowke, Vernon C. *The National Policy and the Wheat Economy.* Toronto: University of Toronto Press, 1957.

Lomborg, Bjorn. *The Skeptical Environmentalist: Measuring the Real State of the World.* Cambridge: Cambridge University Press, 2001.

Lowe, Peter. *Amazon Colonists: Family Photographs from the Ecuadorian Amazon.* Quito, Ecuador: Fundacion Nanpaz, 1999.

McDougall, John N. *Fuels and the National Policy.* Toronto: Butterworths, 1982.

McKenzie-Brown, Peter, Gordon Jaremko, and David Finch. *The Great Oil Age.* Calgary: Detselig Enterprises Ltd., 1993.

Newman, Peter C. *Titans: How the New Canadian Establishment Seized Power.* Toronto: Penguin Books Canada, 1998.

Nikiforuk, Andrew. *Saboteurs: Wiebo Ludwig's War Against Big Oil.* Toronto: Macfarlane Walter & Ross, 2001.

Rasmussen, Linda, Lorna Rasmussen, Candace Savage, and Anne Wheeler. *A Harvest Yet to Reap: A History of Prairie Women.* Toronto: The Women's Press, 1976.

Sharpe, Sydney, and Don Braid. *Storming Babylon: Preston Manning and the Rise of the Reform Party.* Toronto: Key Porter Books, 1992.

Sharpe, Sydney, and Natalie Sharpe. "Subsistence Versus Subservience: A Study of the Socio-economic Framework of the National Policy and the Basis of Land Tenure as it Exists Today for Metis and Farmers in Western Canada." In *Origins of the Alberta Metis: Land Claims Research.* Edmonton: Metis Association of Alberta, and Ottawa: Native Council of Canada, 1978.

Stacey, E.C. *Beaverlodge to the Rockies.* Beaverlodge, Alberta: Beaverlodge and District Historical Association, 1974.

Stenson, Fred. *Waste to Wealth: A History of Gas Processing in Canada.* Calgary: Canadian Gas Processors Association, 1985.

Wood, David G. *The Lougheed Legacy.* Toronto: Key Porter Books, 1985.

Correspondence

Comartin, Joe, MP. "When you think of Canada's environment, what worries you most?" Form letter. New Democratic Party of Canada. March 2002.

Dickey, Peter. "Nomination for Barry Worbets as an individual in the Corporate or Institutional Leadership Category." Emerald Awards. April 10, 2002.

Simpson, Jim, Chairman, Canadian Association of Petroleum Producers (CAPP). Letter to the Honourable Herb Dhaliwal, Minister of Natural Resources, and to the Honourable David Anderson, Minister of the Environment, House of Commons. June 26, 2002.

Government and Regulatory Publications

Alberta Energy and Utilities Board (EUB). "Appendix 1—EUB Policy and Technical Guidelines." *EUB Guide 56: Energy Development Application Guide,* Volume 2. October 2000. http://www.eub.gov.ab.ca/bbs/products/guides/g56-v2.pdf

———. *Enforcement Brochure.* May 9, 2000. http://www.eub.gov.ab.ca/BBS/enforcement/EnforcementBrochure/Enfo rcementBrochure.htm

———. *EUB Guide 56: Energy Development Application Guide,* Volume 1. Oct. 2000. http://www.eub.gov.ab.ca/bbs/products/guides/g56-v1.pdf

———. *Informational Letter IL 2001-1: Appropriate Dispute Resolution (ADR) Program and Guidelines for Energy Industry Disputes.* January 8, 2001. http://www.eub.gov.ab.ca/bbs/ils/ils/il2001-01.htm

———. *Informational Letter IL 99-4-Clarification: EUB Enforcement Process—Clarification.* February 24, 2000. http://www.eub.gov.ab.ca/BBS/ils/ils/il99-04.htm

———. *Informational Letter IL 99-4: EUB Enforcement Process, Generic Enforcement Ladder, and Field Surveillance Enforcement Ladder.* June 8, 1999. http://www.eub.gov.ab.ca/BBS/ils/ils/il99-04.htm

———. *Public Safety and Sour Gas Implementation Plan, Quarterly Progress Report, July–September 2001.* October 26, 2001. http://www.eub.gov.ab.ca/bbs/public/sourgas/qr-2001-10.pdf

———. *Response to Inquiry Request from the Ludwig, Schilthuis, Boonstra, Wraight, Bryzgorni, and Johnstone Families and Dr. W.O. Scott.* May 9, 2000.

———. *Statistical Series 57: Field Surveillance Provincial Summaries.* April 1999/March 2000.

———. *Upstream Petroleum Industry Flaring Report for Year Ending December 31, 2000.* July 2001. http://www.eub.gov.ab.ca/bbs/products/STs/st60b-2001.pdf

Alberta Human Resources and Employment. *Workplace Health & Safety: Hydrogen Sulphide.* Edmonton: July 1998.

Alberta Occupational Health and Safety. *H_2S: "The Killer."* Edmonton: 1988.

News Releases, Backgrounders, and Other Media Materials

Alberta Energy and Utilities Board (EUB) Committee on Public Safety and Sour Gas. "Provincial Advisory Committee on Public Safety and Sour Gas Releases Final Report: Findings and Recommendations." News release. December 18, 2000.

———. "EUB Action on Ludwig Inquiry Request." News release. April 20, 2000.

Alberta Energy Company Ltd. (AEC). "Conflict Resolution." AEC document. No date.

———. AEC West–Saddle Hills Awareness Committee. "Working with the Community." Backgrounder. Alberta Energy Company Ltd., no date.

———. "AEC Environmental Record." Backgrounder. Alberta Energy Company Ltd., no date.

———. "AEC West Gas Processing Plants—'Protecting the Environment.'" Backgrounder. Alberta Energy Company Ltd., no date.

———. "AEC West Hythe Plant—'A Commitment to Environment and Community.'" Backgrounder. Alberta Energy Company Ltd., no date.

———. "AEC West Ombudsman—'Serving the Community.'" Backgrounder. Alberta Energy Company Ltd., no date.

———. "AEC West Reduces Solution Gas Flaring 50%—'Already Meets Clean Air Strategic Alliance Target for 2003.'" Backgrounder. Alberta Energy Company Ltd., no date.

———. "AEC West Sexsmith Plant—'Most Advanced in the Industry.'" Backgrounder. Alberta Energy Company Ltd., no date.

Alberta Environmental Protection. "Air Quality Monitoring in the County of Grande Prairie, December 1 to 15, 1998." Alberta Environmental Protection report, no date.

Borstad, Roy, and Dick Wilson. "County, Alberta Energy Company Team Up to Help Residents 'Take Back Their Community.'" AEC news release, September 14, 1998.

Canadian Association of Petroleum Producers (CAPP). "Aggressive Plan Addresses Sour Gas Issues." CAPP, January 17, 2002.

———. "New Appropriate Dispute Resolution Process Working for Landowners and Energy Industry." CAPP, January 17, 2002.

———. "Petroleum Industry Surpasses Flaring Reduction Targets across Alberta." CAPP, January 17, 2002.

Clean Air Strategic Alliance (CASA). "CASA Begins Work on Air Emissions Management Approach for Electricity Sector." News release. March 8, 2002.

EnCana Corporation. "EnCana Corporation Launches Operations." News release. April 8, 2002.

McGillivray, E.J., and Alan M. Johnston. "With a Gas Plant as your Neighbour . . ." Alberta Energy Company Ltd. document, September 14, 1998.

Morgan, Gwyn, Ed McGillivray, and Dick Wilson. "AEC: Industrial Terrorism, a Creeping Sickness That Must Be Eradicated." AEC news release, September 14, 1998.

Rife Resources Ltd. "Media Release." News release re: Grande Prairie landowner's complaint. January 26, 1999.

Western Interprovincial Scientific Studies Association. "Western Interprovincial Scientific Studies Association Releases Research Designs of Western Canada Study on Animal and Human Health." News release. November 19, 2001.

Newspaper and Magazine Articles

Alberta Venture. "Most Respected Corporations 2001." *Alberta Venture.* May 2001.

Anderson, David. "Certain warming." Letter to the Editor. *Calgary Herald,* June 11, 2002.

Associated Press. "Australia refuses to ratify Kyoto Accord." *Calgary Herald,* June 6, 2002.

———. "Warming could be a natural cycle: Study." *Calgary Herald,* March 22, 2002.

Bannerjee, Neela. "Oil industry hesitates over move into Arctic." *New York Times,* March 10, 2002.

Baxter, James. "Anderson casts doubt on Kyoto ratification." *Calgary Herald,* March 19, 2002.

Bergman, Brian. "Disturbing the Peace." *Maclean's,* February 8, 1999.

———. "Oil, Gas and the Environment Produce a Potent Mixture in Peace River Country." *Maclean's,* February 8, 1999.

Blatchford, Christie. "Wiebo's dynamite." *National Post,* April 8, 2000.

Beauchesne, Eric. "Transfers to have-nots neutralize oil advantage." *National Post,* August 1, 2002.

Braid, Don. "Lougheed urges Kyoto fight." *Calgary Herald,* September 1, 2002.

Bott, Robert. "True Grit: How Syncrude Manages for Success." *Report on Business Magazine,* May 1995.

Brean, Joseph. "Time to colonize Mars, ecologists say." *National Post,* July 9, 2002.

Brethour, Patrick. "Power of oil as a weapon deemed myth." *Globe and Mail,* May 6, 2002.

Brimble, Shelley. "Speaking Editorially: Only an Idiot Would Bomb a Sour Gas Pipeline." *Oil & Gas Inquire,* September 1998.

Buchan, David. "First carbon swaps in Europe." *National Post,* May 7, 2002.

Bueckert, Dennis. "Ottawa lays out climate change options, says Kyoto Protocol affordable." *National Post Online,* May 16, 2002.

Calgary Herald. "Natural Gas: Achieving Balance—A Special Report." *Calgary Herald,* March 4, 2002.

Canadian Press. "Canada's Kyoto hesitance scolded." *Calgary Herald,* March 16, 2002.

———. "Ludwig 'sniffer bus' to monitor oilpatch emissions." *Calgary Herald,* July 13, 2002.

———. "Oilpatch halts 50% of toxic flaring." *Calgary Herald,* May 8, 2002.

———. "Study points to N.S. oil and gas boom." *Calgary Herald,* June 6, 2002.

Cattaneo, Claudia. "How oil became everyone's obsession." *Financial Post,* April 22, 2002.

Chase, Steven. "Kyoto impact estimates vary widely." *Globe and Mail,* April 26, 2002.

Chase, Steven, and Heather Scoffield. "Canada develops alternatives to Kyoto, Rock says." *Globe and Mail*, May 7, 2002.

Cleland, Mike. "Price may outweigh reduced emissions." *Calgary Herald*, April 6, 2002.

Climate Change Central. "To Kyoto or Not to Kyoto. Is This the Question?" *C3 Views*, February 2002.

Collison, Melanie. "Midstream Gains." *Oilweek*, February 4, 2002.

———. "Sore Spot—Environmental Services Harnessed on Large Scale to Try Solving Sour Gas Puzzle." *Oilweek*, March 4, 2002.

Corcoran, Terence. "Scare masters." *Financial Post*, March 2, 2002.

Cotter, John. "Alta climate change plan calls for billions for technology research." *National Post Online*, May 16, 2002.

Creighton, Jayne. "In Fighting Form: AEC's Strong Man Gwyn Morgan Goes Toe-to-Toe with Industrial Terrorism." *Alberta Venture*, May 1999.

Dawson, Deborah. "At Your Disposal: Second-to-None Environmental Regulation Sires Thriving Specialties." *Oilweek*, May 6, 2002.

Doran, D'Arcy. "Women in Nigerian oil siege win jobs, electricity." *National Post*, July 16, 2002.

Edmonton Journal/Calgary Herald. "Fort McMurray Economic Report." Supplement. *National Post*, May 10, 2002.

Ferguson, Eva. "Klein cools off on Kyoto challenge." *Calgary Herald*, April 19, 2002.

Financial Post. "Taking a courageous stand against industrial terrorism." FP Editorial. *Financial Post*, September 9, 1998.

———. "Apocalypse not." FP Editorial. *Financial Post*, March 12, 2002.

———. "Kyoto's false appeal." FP Editorial. *Financial Post*, June 11, 2002.

Francis, Diane. "Kyoto Accord a bad deal for Canada: Emissions pact commitment should match Australia's." *Financial Post*, March 12, 2002.

Frank, Charles. "Dhaliwal's speech underwhelming." *Calgary Herald*, June 18, 2002.

———. "Ethical issues bubble over." *Calgary Herald*, May 31, 2002.

———. "Options outline horrible costs of Kyoto." *Calgary Herald*, May 16, 2002.

Georg, Anne. "Age of Distrust." *Oilweek*, March 4, 2002.

Globe and Mail. "Tackling Climate Change: Will Canada Profit by Emissions Reduction?" Supplement. *Globe and Mail*, May 16, 2002.

Goodspeed, Peter. "Nigerian women seize oil terminal." *National Post*, July 12, 2002.

Goold, Douglas. "The Environment Is under Attack, but There Is Hope. We May Be Headed to a Pollution-free Hydrogen Economy." *R.O.B. Magazine*, May 2002.

Haggett, Scott. "Alberta on brink of energy showdown." *Calgary Herald*, May 23, 2002.

———. "Kyoto signing by end of year: Dhaliwal." *Calgary Herald*, June 18, 2002.

———. "North edges East Coast as favoured drilling site." *Calgary Herald*, July 5, 2002.

———. "A world class contribution to business." *Calgary Herald*, July 3, 2002.

Hart, Lee. "Oil Industry Impact Studied." *Alberta Crops & Beef.* March 4, 2002.

Heinrich, Susan. "Sunoco showcasing its greener side." *Financial Post,* June 3, 2002.

Howes, Carol. "Canada won't sign Kyoto: Peterson." *Financial Post,* March 13, 2002.

Jaremko, Gordon. "Direct Approach: Sour Gas Taste Test in the Works." *Oilweek,* March 4, 2002.

Kenny, Andrew. "Global warning—prepare for the big chill." *National Post,* July 9, 2002.

Koch, George. "The Wiebo Ludwig saga." *Calgary Herald,* July 2, 1999.

Lambie, Chris, and Kate Jaimet. "Global warming has economic upside, federal minister says." *National Post,* May 15, 2002.

Lau, Michael. "Huge success of event leads to big plans for 2004." *Calgary Herald,* June 14, 2002.

Leiss, William, and Stephen Hill. "How the Feds could convince Alberta to buy Kyoto." *Calgary Herald,* June 10, 2002.

Levine, Mark. "The Souring of the Good Reverend's Nature." *Outside Magazine,* December 1998.

Lindzen, Richard S. "Scientists' report doesn't support the Kyoto Treaty." *Wall Street Journal,* June 11, 2001.

Lorenz, Andrea. "Ambassadors of Industry: Book Chronicles Role of Landmen (and, since 1974, Women)." *Oilweek,* May 6, 2002, p. 12.

———. "Permanent Crisis: Tracing a U.S. Pattern in Energy Decision-making." *Oilweek,* March 4, 2002.

Lowey, Mark. "CAPP Draws Green Line for Membership—Environmental Stewardship Rules Now Mandatory for Producers." *Business Edge,* June 27–July 10, 2002.

———. "Industry Backs Sour Gas Tests on Volunteers." *Business Edge,* March 28–April 3, 2002.

———. "Oilpatch and Agriculture in Water Fight." *Business Edge,* August 22–September 4, 2002.

———. "Report Touts Kyoto Benefits to Oil Industry." *Business Edge,* June 20–26, 2002.

MacRae, Allan. "Reject the Kyoto scam." *National Post,* August 1, 2002.

Maloney, Tom. "Disbelief clouds climate science." *Calgary Herald,* April 8, 2002.

———. "Canadians told to park their SUVs: Germany joins in criticism of Accord stance." *Calgary Herald,* April 15, 2002.

Marr, Garry. "Kyoto's chances down to 50%, executives say." *Financial Post,* May 20, 2002.

Martin, Don. "Rock signals Cabinet split on Kyoto Accord." *National Post,* April 3, 2002.

———. "The climate change Accord: A trial balloon that just burst." *Calgary Herald,* May 16, 2002.

McIntyre, Barry. "Mars heats up." Letter to the Editor. *Calgary Herald,* June 10, 2002.

McKitrick, Ross. "Political 'science.'" *Financial Post,* April 6, 2002.

Menzies, Peter. "Kyoto myths cloud the debate." *Calgary Herald,* June 6, 2002.

Michaels, Patrick J. "Look who's isolated on Kyoto." *Financial Post,* April 29, 2002.

Mills, Bob. "This man doesn't want to see you today." *Calgary Herald,* June 14, 2002.

Mittelstaedt, Martin. "Effects of warming 'clearly visible.'" *Globe and Mail,* March 27, 2002.

Mofina, Rick, and Tom Olsen. "Public shut out of Kyoto talks." *Calgary Herald,* June 7, 2002.

Munro, Margaret. "Fossils show tropical plants grew in Arctic." *National Post,* June 7, 2002.

Newell, Eric P. "Canada's Oilsands Industry Comes of Age." *Oil & Gas Journal,* June 28, 1999.

Nguyen, Lily. "'Agnostic' oil patch seeks Kyoto clarity." *Globe and Mail,* March 16, 2002.

———. "Coal firms to pitch research project." *Globe and Mail,* March 11, 2002.

Nickle's Daily Oil Bulletin. "Federal plan sparks renewed Kyoto debate." *Nickle's Daily Oil Bulletin,* May 15, 2002.

Nikiforuk, Andrew. "Water Fight." *National Post Business,* July 2002.

Oilweek. "Fighting the Squeeze Between Greenhouse Gas Attacks and Aging Wells." *Oilweek,* May 6, 2002.

Olsen, Tom. "Alberta commits to Kyoto targets." *Calgary Herald,* May 8, 2002.

———. "Klein compares Protocol to Trudeau-era policy." *Calgary Herald,* June 14, 2002.

———. "Special fund may finance Fort McMurray growth." *Calgary Herald,* June 13, 2002.

Palmer, Randall. "Canada won't decide on Kyoto by Earth Summit." *Financial Post,* August 10, 2002.

Patterson, Tim. "Climate change is nothing new." *National Post,* July 15, 2002.

Petroleum Communication Foundation. "Albertans Rate the Petroleum Industry." *Connexions,* Fall 1999.

Reguly, Eric. "Economic fear-mongering protects the gas guzzlers." *Globe and Mail,* March 16, 2002.

Remington, Robert. "Kyoto's doubters allege bias in funding." *National Post,* April 3, 2002.

Reuters, Associated Press. "Australia rejects Kyoto, claims pact doomed." *National Post,* June 6, 2002.

Rheaume, Gilles. "A New Spirit of Partnership: An Interview with Eric P. Newell, Chairman, President and CEO, Syncrude Canada Ltd." Reprint. *Canadian Business Review,* Summer 1994.

Robertson, Grant, and Chris Varcoe. "Industry frustrated by lack of closure." *Calgary Herald,* May 16, 2002.

Scotton, Geoffrey. "N.W.T. Premier urges 'tough love' with U.S." *Calgary Herald*, May 7, 2002.

———. "U.S. energy mission aims to reduce differences." *Calgary Herald*, May 8, 2002.

Seeman, Neil. "Polar bear scares." *Financial Post*, June 22, 2002.

Seskus, Tony. "Oilpatch pits hopes on North." *Financial Post*, July 5, 2002.

———. "Oil industry using too much water, farmers say." *Financial Post*, August 10, 2002.

Seskus, Tony, and Claudia Cattaneo. "U.S. energy firms join fight against Senate bill." *Financial Post*, May 7, 2002.

Seskus, Tony, and Alan Toulin. "Alberta blasts Anderson for Kyoto switch." *National Post*, May 23, 2002.

Sharpe, Sydney. "Now will the bombings stop?" *Calgary Sun*, January 17, 1999. See also other Page Two columns on Wiebo Ludwig in the *Calgary Sun*, January 30, June 23, and September 22, 1999.

Shirley, Clive, and Leslie Jermyn. "Outrage in the Rainforest." *Maclean's*, July 29, 2002.

Smith, Audrey. "Doom doubted." Letter to the Editor. *Calgary Herald*, June 11, 2002.

Solomon, Lawrence. "Climate change theory ca. 1887." *Financial Post*, June 22, 2002.

Spears, Tom. "Chilly spring ends warm streak." *Calgary Herald*, June 7, 2002.

Staples, David. "A harsh shepherd: Of faith and fury." *Edmonton Journal*, December 11, 1999.

———. "Trouble at Trickle Creek." *Edmonton Journal*, December 12, 1999.

Stenson, Fred. "Big Oil vs. Landowners." *Alberta Views*, May/June 2002.

Stevenson, James. "Ottawa's intentions to pursue Kyoto ratification sends chill through oilpatch." *National Post Online*, May 16, 2002.

Struzik, Ed. "Mackenzie pipeline a boon for economy: Study." *National Post*, April 5, 2002.

Suzuki, David. "Suzuki believes Alberta will benefit from Kyoto." *Calgary Herald*, May 16, 2002.

Toulin, Alan. "Alberta offers Kyoto alternative." *Financial Post*, March 28, 2002.

———. "Alberta quits Kyoto negotiation." *National Post*, May 22, 2002.

———. "Drivers attack Kyoto toll plan." *Financial Post*, June 7, 2002.

———. "Environment key part of power equation: Report." *Financial Post*, June 18, 2002.

———. "Kyoto benefits could bypass Canada: Report." *Financial Post*, March 18, 2002.

———. "Kyoto support a world away." *National Post*, May 20, 2002.

———. "Kyoto possible without hurting economy: CEOs." *National Post*, July 30, 2002.

———. "No easy road to Kyoto." *National Post*, May 16, 2002.

Toulin, Alan, and Robert Benzie. "Harris ups anti-Kyoto pressure." *Financial Post*, April 5, 2002.

Usborne, David. "War in Peace country." *The Independent*, December 8, 1998.

Varcoe, Chris. "Abandon Kyoto, CEOs urge." *Calgary Herald*, June 21, 2002.

Verburg, Peter. "Land of the Giant: The Making of Encana." *Canadian Business*, April 15, 2002.

Watson, William. "Kyoto's empty black box." Editorial. *Financial Post*, April 3, 2002.

———. "Parched Alberta should price its water." *Financial Post*, July 5, 2002.

Weaver, Alan. "Changing energy use can be beneficial." *Calgary Herald*, April 6, 2002.

Weber, Bob. "Berger Commission's impact still being felt 25 years later." *Calgary Herald*, June 20, 2002.

Willis, Andrew. "Canadians don't trust executives, survey says." *Globe and Mail*, July 2, 2002.

Wilson, Kathleen Laverty. "Arctic Thaw: Us-and-Them Barrier Melted by Pioneer Partnerships with Natives." *Oilweek*, May 6, 2002.

Yedlin, Deborah. "Bottom-line focus doesn't always pay." *Calgary Herald*, June 14, 2002.

Reports and Papers

Bietz, Brian F. "Reengineering Regulation: Goals and Opportunities." Charlottetown: Energy Council of Canada Forum '96, May 27–28, 1996.

Bramley, Matthew. "A Comparison of Current Government Action on Climate Change in the U.S. and Canada." Drayton Valley, Alberta: Pembina Institute and World Wildlife Fund Canada, May 2002.

Brenneman, Ron. *Petro-Canada Report to the Community.* Calgary: Petro-Canada, no date.

Canadian Association of Petroleum Producers (CAPP) and Small Explorers and Producers Association of Canada (SEPAC). "Action on Energy: A Progress Report from Alberta's Oil and Gas Industry." Calgary: CAPP/SEPAC, 2001.

———. *2001 Environment, Health and Safety Stewardship Progress Report—Building Momentum.* Calgary: CAPP, December 2001.

———. "CAPP Input to June 14th Workshop on Federal Climate Change Policy: Technical Backgrounder." Calgary: CAPP, June 14, 2002.

———. "Climate Change: The Upstream Oil and Natural Gas Industry's Contribution to Canada's Debate on Climate Change and the Kyoto Protocol." Calgary: CAPP, February 2002.

———. "First Nations Issues." Calgary: CAPP, March 20, 2002.

Clean Air Strategic Alliance (CASA). "Assessment of Respiratory Disorders in Relation to Solution Gas Flaring Activities in Alberta." Edmonton: CASA, February 1998.

Dawson, C.A. Unpublished notes. Edmonton: University of Alberta, Bruce Peel Special Collections, Books 1, 2, and 3.

Faris, Dawn. "The Effect of Social and Technological Change upon the Role of the Housewife in the Peace River Country." Unpublished paper. Grande Prairie Junior College, 1968.

Faithfull, Tim. *Progress Toward Sustainable Development—2000 Sustainable Development Report.* Calgary: Shell Canada Ltd., April 2001.

Gossen, Randall G., Garry J. Mann, and Laura de Jonge. "Integrating Corporate Social Responsibility into a Corporate Culture, the Quest to Embed Integrity into the Workplace." Paper presented at the Society of Petroleum Engineers International Conference on Health, Safety and Environment in Oil and Gas Exploration and Production. Kuala Lumpur, Malaysia, March 2002.

Hydrogeological Consultants Ltd. "Use of Water by the Upstream Oil and Gas Industry." Prepared for Canadian Association of Petroleum Producers (CAPP). Calgary: March 2002.

Mansell, R.L. "A Socio-Economic Survey of Isolated Communities in Northern Alberta." Government of Alberta, Human Resources Development Authority. Edmonton: July 1970.

Nexen Inc. *Bringing Value to the Surface: Annual Report 2001.* Calgary: Nexen, 2002.

———. *Safety, Environment & Social Responsibility—Annual Report 2001.* Calgary: Nexen, February 7, 2002.

Pembina Institute for Appropriate Development. "Pembina Institute Perspective on Climate Change." Drayton Valley, Alberta: Pembina Institute, April 2002.

Shell Canada Limited. *2001 Annual Report.* Calgary: Shell, March 2002.

Shell International 2001 Global Business Environment. *Energy Needs, Choices and Possibilities: Scenarios to 2050.* Royal Dutch/Shell Group. London: Shell International Ltd., 2001.

Suncor Energy Inc. *Our Journey Toward Sustainable Development—2001 Report on Sustainability.* Calgary: Suncor, September 2001.

———. *Recognize the Energy Difference—2001 Annual Report.* Calgary: Suncor, January 16, 2002.

Syncrude Canada Ltd. "Aboriginal Review—A Report on the Relationship Between Syncrude Canada Ltd. and the Aboriginal People of Northeastern Alberta." Fort McMurray: Syncrude, no date.

———. "Aboriginal Review 1997." Fort McMurray: Syncrude, no date.

———. "Environmental Innovation—Securing Sustainable Development." Fort McMurray: Syncrude, no date.

———. "Environmental Progress Summary 1999." Fort McMurray: Syncrude, no date.

———. "Syncrude Canada Climate Change Voluntary Challenge Action Plan 1996." Fort McMurray: Syncrude, no date.

———. "Syncrude Takes Action—A Summary of Syncrude's 1997 Climate Change Voluntary Challenge Action Plan." Fort McMurray: Syncrude, no date.

Speeches and Presentations

Bietz, Brian, and John Kingsbury. "Virtual Processing—An Emerging Trend." CGPA/PJVA Joint Conference, November 1, 2002.

Canadian Association of Petroleum Producers (CAPP). "The Canadian Oil and Natural Gas Industry—Industry Profile." Calgary: CAPP, no date.

Eastlick, Kim. "EUB Guide 60—A Sneak Preview." Presentation to CGPA/CGPSA second quarterly meeting. Edmonton: Alberta Energy and Utilities Board (EUB), May 14, 2002.

Kakfwi, Stephen. Speech to Annual Dinner of the Canadian Association of Petroleum Producers. Calgary, April 18, 2002.

Klein, Ralph. Speaking Notes for Premier Ralph Klein—Calgary Premiers' Dinner. Calgary, April 4, 2002.

Marr-Laing, Tom. "The Basis of Landowner Concerns Relating to Gas Flaring." Calgary: Centrum Conference: Dealing with New Gas Flaring Rules, September 25, 2001.

McCrank, Neil. "Building on Today's Success: The Challenge for Tomorrow." Making Synergy Real Conference, February 26, 2002.

———. "Access to Land Issues—Through the Regulatory Process." Vancouver: Canadian Association of Landmen Conference, September 26, 2001.

Morgan, Gwyn. "Remarks by Gwyn Morgan, President & CEO Alberta Energy Company Ltd." Calgary, February 8, 1999.

———. "Terrorism and a Fractured Community." News conference remarks. Calgary, September 14, 1998.

———. "A Canadian Global Champion—Welcome Address to Employees of EnCana Corporation." Calgary, April 8, 2002.

———. "Remarks to the Canadian Newspapers Super Conference, Panel Discussion." Calgary, April 25, 2002.

Newell, Eric P. "Leadership in the 21st Century." Waterloo: Laurier Outstanding Business Leader of the Year Luncheon, June 7, 2001.

———. "Putting People First: The Surest Route to Success in Business." Calgary: First Canadian Open Business Forum—Building Corporate Social and Environmental Responsibility, March 8, 2001.

Worbets, Barry. "Conservation Biology and Implications for Policy." NRTEE Workshop, July 4, 2001.

Statutes and Regulations

Alberta *Occupational Health and Safety Act* (O-2 RSA 2000).

Chemical Hazards Regulation (Alberta Regulation 393/88). *Occupational Health and Safety Act.*

Energy Resources Conservation Act (RSA 1980), Chap. E-11.

General Safety Regulation (Alberta Regulation 448/83). *Occupational Health and Safety Act.*

Web Sites

Web sites relating to oil and gas and the environment are vast in number and extremely useful, but they are also dynamic by their nature. Consequently, some references may no longer contain the information cited. For this reason only a few sites that were used are named here.

Alberta Energy and Utilities Board. "Appropriate Dispute Resolution (ADR)." Updated April 11, 2001. http://www.eub.gov.ab.ca/bbs/public/adr/index.htm

Clean Air Strategic Alliance (CASA). "Airsheds Directory." Updated March 13, 2002. http://www.casahome.org/about_casa/directory/airshed_direct.asp

———. "Airsheds." Updated March 13, 2002. http://www.casahome.org/airshed.zones/index.asp

———. "Alberta Symposium on Air Quality and Health State of the Science." Updated March 13, 2002. http://www.casahome.org/for_albertans/symposiumprogram.asp

———. "What Is Consensus?" Updated March 13, 2002. http://www.casahome.org/about_casa/CONSENSUS.ASP

CNN.com./SPACE. "Sun Farther Away but Earth Hotter." Posted July 5, 2002. http://www.cnn.com/2002/TECH/space/07/05/earth.sun/index.html

David Suzuki Foundation. http://www.davidsuzuki.org/

Energy Information Administration. "Canada: Environmental Issues." Accessed April 11, 2002. http://www.eia.doe.gov/cabs/canenv.html

Global Reporting Initiative (GRI). "What Is GRI?" Accessed April 10, 2002. http://www.globalreporting.org/

Imagine. "What Is Imagine?" Accessed April 17, 2002. http://www.imagine.ca/

The Nisga'a. "The Sparrow Decision." Accessed May 30, 2002. http://www.ntc.bc.ca/no_frames/sparrow.html

Sogapro Engineering Ltd. "Serving the International Sour Gas Industry." Accessed February 14, 2002. http://www.sogapro.com

United Nations Framework on Climate Change. "Text of the Kyoto Protocol." Accessed July 19, 2002. http://unfccc.int/resource/docs/convkp/kpeng.html

———. "The Convention and Kyoto Protocol." Accessed July 19, 2002. http://unfccc.int/resource/convkp.html#kp

World Business Council for Sustainable Development. "The Business Case for Sustainable Development: Making a Difference Toward the Johannesburg Summit 2002 and Beyond." Accessed July 19, 2002. http://www.wbcsd.org

Index